Genghis Khan's Mongol Empire

Other titles in the *Lost Civilizations* series include:

The Ancient Egyptians
The Ancient Greeks
The Ancient Persians
The Ancient Romans
The Aztecs
The Celts
The Etruscans
The Han Dynasty
The Inca
The Mayans
The Minoans
The Vikings

LOST CIVILIZATIONS

GENGHIS KHAN'S
MONGOL
EMPIRE

Tom Streissguth

LUCENT BOOKS

An imprint of Thomson Gale, a part of The Thomson Corporation

Detroit • New York • San Francisco • San Diego • New Haven, Conn. • Waterville, Maine • London • Munich

LIBRARY OF CONGRESS CATALOGING-IN-PUBLICATION DATA

Streissguth, Thomas, 1958–
  Genghis Khan's Mongol empire / by Tom Streissguth.
    p. cm. — (Lost civilizations)
  Audience: Grades 7–8.
  Includes bibliographical references.
  ISBN 1-59018-436-X (hard cover : alk. paper)
  1. Mongols—History—To 1500—Juvenile literature. 2. Genghis Khan, 1162–1227—Juvenile literature. I. Title. II. Series: Lost civilizations (San Diego, Calif.)
  DS19.S825 2005
  950'.2—dc22
                                                        2004028220

Printed in the United States of America

CONTENTS

FOREWORD

"What marvel is this?" asked the noted eighteenth-century German poet and philosopher, Friedrich Schiller. "O earth . . . what is your lap sending forth? Is there life in the deeps as well? A race yet unknown hiding under the lava?" The "marvel" that excited Schiller was the discovery, in the early 1700s, of two entire ancient Roman cities buried beneath over 60 feet (18m) of hardened volcanic ash and lava near the modern city of Naples, on Italy's western coast. "Ancient Pompeii is found again!" Schiller joyfully exclaimed. "And the city of Hercules rises!"

People had known about the existence of long-lost civilizations before Schiller's day, of course. Stonehenge, a circle of huge, very ancient stones had stood, silent and mysterious, on a plain in Britain as long as people could remember. And the ruins of temples and other structures erected by the ancient inhabitants of Egypt, Palestine, Greece, and Rome had for untold centuries sprawled in magnificent profusion throughout the Mediterranean world. But when, why, and how were these monuments built? And what were the exact histories and beliefs of the peoples who built them? A few scattered surviving ancient literary texts had provided some partial answers to some of these questions. But not until Pompeii and Herculaneum started to emerge from the ashes did the modern world begin to study and reconstruct lost civilizations in a systematic manner.

Even then, the process was at first slow and uncertain. Pompeii, a bustling, prosperous town of some twenty thousand inhabitants, and the smaller Herculaneum met their doom on August 24, A.D. 79, when the nearby volcano, Mt. Vesuvius, blew its top and literally erased them from the map. For nearly seventeen centuries, their contents, preserved in a massive cocoon of volcanic debris, rested undisturbed. Not until the early eighteenth century did people begin raising statues and other artifacts from the buried cities; and at first this was done in a haphazard, unscientific manner. The diggers, who were seeking art treasures to adorn their gardens and mansions, gave no thought to the historical value of the finds. The sad fact was that at the time no trained experts existed to dig up and study lost civilizations in a proper manner.

This unfortunate situation began to change in 1763. In that year, Johann J. Winckelmann, a German librarian fascinated by antiquities (the name then used for ancient artifacts), began to investigate Pompeii and Herculaneum. Although he made some mistakes and drew some wrong conclusions, Winckelmann laid the initial, crucial groundwork for a new science—archaeology (a term derived from two Greek words meaning "to talk about ancient things").

His book, *History of the Art of Antiquity*, became a model for the first generation of archaeologists to follow in their efforts to understand other lost civilizations. "With unerring sensitivity," noted scholar C.W. Ceram explains, "Winckelmann groped toward original insights, and expressed them with such power of language that the cultured European world was carried away by a wave of enthusiasm for the antique ideal. This . . . was of prime importance in shaping the course of archaeology in the following century. It demonstrated means of understanding ancient cultures through their artifacts."

In the two centuries that followed, archaeologists, historians, and other scholars began to piece together the remains of lost civilizations around the world. The glory that was Greece, the grandeur that was Rome, the cradles of human civilization in Egypt's Nile valley and Mesopotamia's Tigris-Euphrates valley, the colorful royal court of ancient China's Han Dynasty, the mysterious stone cities of the Maya and Aztecs in Central America—all of these

and many more were revealed in fascinating, often startling, if sometimes incomplete, detail by the romantic adventure of archaeological research. This work, which continues, is vital. "Digs are in progress all over the world," says Ceram. "For we need to understand the past five thousand years in order to master the next hundred years."

Each volume in the Lost Civilizations series examines the history, works, everyday life, and importance of ancient cultures. The archaeological discoveries and methods used to gather this knowledge are stressed throughout. Where possible, quotes by the ancients themselves, and also by later historians, archaeologists, and other experts support and enliven the text. Primary and secondary sources are carefully documented by footnotes and each volume supplies the reader with an extensive Works Consulted list. These and other research tools afford the reader a thorough understanding of how a civilization that was long lost has once more seen the light of day and begun to reveal its secrets to its captivated modern descendants.

AN EMPIRE OF NOMADS

In the early thirteenth century, the Mongol army spread terror across much of Asia. With Genghis Khan leading them, the Mongols marched out of their homeland in northeastern Asia and destroyed entire nations. Cities that resisted were conquered and their people massacred. The Mongols rode from China to Iraq to the Caucasus Mountains, winning every battle they fought.

There was simply no defense against Genghis Khan's army. The Mongols were disciplined, tough nomads who were accustomed to living in a very harsh climate. These soldiers fought skillfully, using arrows, lances, battle-axes, and tactics of deception and surprise to demoralize their enemies. They used catapults and underground mines to bring down the strongest city walls. As news of the Mongol invasions spread across Asia, entire armies fled or simply laid down their arms before battle could begin.

Under Genghis Khan's leadership, the Mongols transformed themselves from a divided and very poor society, with no industry or agriculture whatsoever, into the most feared people on earth. They conquered northern China, central Asia, the caliphate of Baghdad, and the principalities of Russia.

After the death of Genghis Khan, they swarmed through Poland and then continued on to Hungary, where they smashed the armies of King Bela IV. After chasing this king to the shores of the Adriatic Sea, they continued to the gates of Vienna, the capital of the Hapsburg Empire.

To those who suffered their assaults, the Mongols were like visitors from hell (their nickname, "Tartars," reminded Europeans of Tartarus, the underworld of ancient Greek mythology). They gave no quarter in battle and rarely showed mercy to civilians, including women and children, artisans, aristocrats, and kings. They represented a destructive force, the antithesis of civilization. Down through history they have been described as the Chinese described them, as barbarians and raiders, a human plague to be dealt with as one deals with wild animals.

Yet there was a Mongol civilization, one based on centuries of myth and oral tradition. The Mongols had transformed themselves from forest-dwelling hunters to nomadic herders, moving with the seasons and dividing themselves into small, independent clans. Conquered nations did not adapt to this culture but in the wake of the Mongol invasions, they did enjoy a period of stability and security. The Mongols

In the thirteenth century, Genghis Khan and his fierce Mongol army swept across Asia, carving out an enormous empire.

fostered trade by protecting the once-dangerous trade routes that linked eastern Asia and the Middle East. They tolerated foreign religions and philosophies and took foreign artisans and scholars into their service. In many ways, these practices of the Mongol realm were an expression of Genghis Khan himself and his notion of a new and better world order.

The Mongol Civilization

The idea of a universal Mongolian realm originated with the most famous and feared Mongol of them all, Genghis Khan. Born as Temuchin, the son of a Mongol chieftain, he survived many years of exile, combat, and captivity to finally attain election as Genghis (universal) Khan (ruler) of the Mongols in 1206.

9

Genghis Khan found his abilities perfectly matched to the task of uniting the Mongol tribes. For twenty-one years, he ruled the Mongols, who saw him as a man of supernatural ability, the founder of their Empire. During his reign, nobody dared challenge his authority or that of his sons and heirs. His legacy was a new code of laws, a system of writing, an effective administration, an unbeatable army, and the largest empire in history.

Genghis Khan saw the Mongol way of life as the best of all possible lives, the ideal to which humanity should aspire. His conquests and laws were meant to bring this ideal to the nomadic tribes of Asia and to the rest of the world. Among his own people, he imposed a system in which every individual had a place, a task, and a prescribed behavior.

Although he saw the Mongol culture as the universal ideal, Genghis Khan welcomed technology and philosophy from outside his borders. He adopted new weapons from the Chinese and the Persians. He allowed Christians, Muslims, and Buddhists to live among his people. He imposed the writing system of the Uighurs, another people of central Asia, on his once-illiterate nation.

At the death of Genghis Khan in 1227, the Mongol Empire covered thousands of miles of tribute-paying lands, from China to central Asia, Persia, and Russia. But there was no way all this territory could become truly "Mongol," populated by and dominated, politically and culturally, by Mongolia. The Mongols could not convert townspeople to nomadism, or turn settled farmers into herders. Russians, Persians, Chinese, and others had cultures and civilizations of their own, which either ignored or overcame Mongol ways. In addition, once

Mongol rulers conquered and settled in new countries, they gave up the nomadic lifestyle of the steppes and lost their fighting edge. Without Genghis Khan to guide and inspire them, they forgot the ideal of a universal Mongolian realm.

For this reason, the Mongol Empire was quite temporary as empires go, lasting only about 150 years. By the end of the fifteenth century, it had disintegrated. The Mongols returned to their original homeland and broke into two large feuding factions. They skirmished with the armies of the Ming dynasty in China, won an occasional battle, and captured a Chinese emperor. But their years of conquest and empire were over.

The Empire's Scant Remains

The Mongols were the last wave of Asian nomads and the last of the world's great migrations. But unlike the Huns, the Celts, the Germans, and other migratory peoples, they never abandoned their ancient traditions to settle down in a new place and take up a new way of life.

For historians and archaeologists, the Mongols represent a fascinating historical puzzle, in which many of the key pieces are missing. The remains of the empire are very scant. The Mongol capital of Karakorum was destroyed by the Chinese in the fifteenth century. The Mongols raised no cities of their own; they lived in round tents made of felt and wood. They built no monuments, cathedrals, towers, or great walls. Only the most illustrious among them were laid to rest in tombs, which were carefully hidden and not marked in any way.

After the decline of the Mongol Empire, many of its artifacts and writings were preserved in Buddhist monasteries. Like all

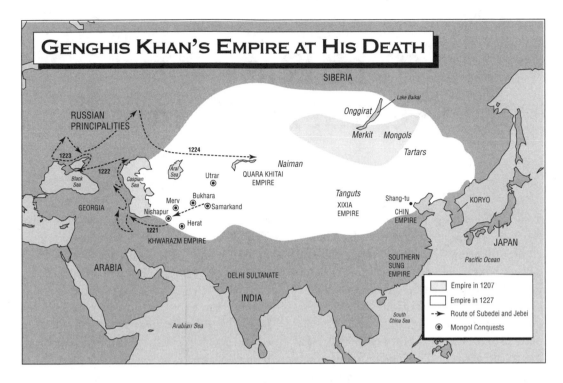

GENGHIS KHAN'S EMPIRE AT HIS DEATH

SIBERIA

Lake Baikal

Onggirat

RUSSIAN PRINCIPALITIES

Merkit Mongols

Tartars

1224

1223

Naiman

1222

Aral Sea

Black Sea

Caspian Sea

Utrar

QUARA KHITAI EMPIRE

Tanguts

Shang-tu

KORYO

GEORGIA

Merv

Bukhara

Samarkand

XIXIA EMPIRE

CHIN EMPIRE

Nishapur

1221

Herat

KHWARAZM EMPIRE

JAPAN

ARABIA

DELHI SULTANATE

Pacific Ocean

SOUTHERN SUNG EMPIRE

INDIA

South China Sea

Arabian Sea

Empire in 1207
Empire in 1227
Route of Subedei and Jebei
Mongol Conquests

other religions, however, Buddhism came under attack in the twentieth century when the Soviet Union and the People's Republic of China imposed a stringent Marxist philosophy against all forms of organized religion. The monasteries were attacked and destroyed, their monks killed or scattered, and their valuable possessions looted.

As a result, the artifacts of Genghis Khan's time remain mostly literary. The life of Genghis Khan was preserved in two important books written by his followers. The *Altan Debter* was a description of Genghis Khan's family and lineages. Although there is no original, a Chinese version dating from 1263, titled *Account of the Campaigns of the Warrior Emperor Saint*, survived the fall of the Mongol Empire. The second original source of Mongol history, the *Secret History of the Mongols*, was also copied and preserved by the Chinese well after the death of Genghis Khan. Historians believe that this book was probably written sometime before 1241, as it recounts only the events of Genghis Khan's reign and that of his son Ogedei. *The Secret History of the Mongols* raises more questions than it answers, however, and the text is so obscure that only experts on Mongol history can even begin to understand it.

But Genghis Khan and the Mongol Empire were not forgotten. For those who encountered them on the battlefield, or from behind high walls and gates, their appearance was a nightmare come true. For students and scholars, the rise and fall of Mongol power—and the accomplishments of Genghis Khan and his army—remain a fascinating enigma, still open to many interpretations and unique in history.

CHAPTER ONE

THE RISE OF GENGHIS KHAN

Today Mongolia is a distant land that lies far from the important routes of trade and communication. The Mongols of Genghis Khan's time lived on a steppe, a region of low hills and grassland, lying east of the Altai and Tien Shan Mountains, north of the Gobi Desert, and south of Siberia. The climate is extreme, with hot, dry summers and long, cold winters. The land provides excellent grazing for livestock but there is little rainfall, making the cultivation of crops and orchards impossible.

For millennia, the steppe tribes had gathered together for raids into northern China. Some of these raids became migrations into central Asia, the plains of Russia, and Europe. The "civilized" worlds of China, the Middle East, and Europe greatly feared the people of the steppes, who appeared as an immense horde, covering the valleys, plains, and cultivated fields of settled peoples like a plague of deadly locusts. The Hsiung-Nu, the most feared of all steppe tribes until the time of the Mongols, forged a powerful confederation in the third century B.C. Known to Europeans as the Huns, the Hsiung-Nu lived as herders, hunters, and raiders. Like the Mongols who came after them, they divided themselves into tribes and clans, each under the command of a chieftain. They wore clothing of hides and skins, survived on raw meat and the milk of their horses and sheep, and lived in tents covered with felt, a thick mat of sheep's wool.

The Hun confederation eventually broke apart, leaving the steppes again a place of scattered, weak tribes. On the northern fringes of this region, a group of clans lived on the frontier between the steppes and the Siberian forests to the north. These people lived as hunters and herders; they raided and fought among themselves and had little contact with the world beyond their homeland. They were people of the forests, not of the desert or steppes, and they imagined their origins in the cold world of the north.

These clans were the ancestors of the Mongols. The other peoples of Mongolia paid them little heed. Until the time of Genghis Khan, the Mongols were divided and weak. On the steppes, strong and charismatic leaders might hold together a short-lived confederation of tribes, but they faced constant challenge from younger men. The nature of Mongol existence also prevented their unity. Roaming from one camp to the next and living in clans united by ties of marriage and family, the Mongols had no use for kings or emperors.

They obeyed only their elders and clan chiefs and lived by traditions passed down orally from one generation to the next. These customs, and their proud independence changed, however, with the rise of Genghis Khan.

A Weak Tribe of Nomads

To the Mongols, Genghis Khan would later personify the best qualities a Mongol could have. These qualities were the attributes of a hunter: patience, endurance, and skill. In the first paragraph of *The Secret History of the Mongols*, an anonymous thirteenth-century author describes the beginnings of the Mongols in the union of a wolf and a deer, the hunter and his prey living along the banks of an inland sea, Lake Baikal:

> There came into the world
>   a blue-gray wolf
>
> whose destiny was Heaven's will.
>
> His wife was a fallow deer.
>
> They travelled across the inland sea
>
> and when they were camped near
>   the source of the Onon River
>
> in sight of Mount Burkhan Khaldun
>
> their first son was born,
>   named Batachikan.[1]

The Hsiung-Nu, or Huns, depicted in this illustration, were nomadic herders, hunters, and raiders from the steppes of Mongolia who terrorized Europe in the time of the late Roman Empire.

THE UIGHUR INFLUENCE

Four centuries after the decline of the Hsiung-Nu confederation in the fourth century, the Uighur Empire rose to power in Mongolia and the Eurasian steppes. The Uighur Turks, who established their first khanate in the fourth century A.D., had their capital in the valley of the Orkhon River, which later became the political heartland of the Mongol empire. They developed a system of writing and followed Buddhism before converting to Islam in the tenth century. The third Uighur khanate broke apart in the ninth century, but survived in the Tarim basin, a desert region in what is now Xinjiang, a remote western province of China.

The Uighurs would have a strong cultural and political influence on the Mongols, who adopted the Uighur script for the writing of their own language. According to historian E.D. Phillips in *The Mongols*,

> Much of the Mongol vocabulary of rule, of social organization, and of military command was taken from the Turks, for they once ruled the Mongols. Examples are: *ordu*, a great camp which was a headquarters or a court; *tumen*, 'ten thousand,' particularly in the military sense of a cavalry division and its recruiting base; *khan*, for a paramount chief, and *khatun* for his wife or other great ladies; *darkhan* for a free man or later a minor chief; *ulus* for a people or group of people.

The Mongols occupied vast steppes that provided grazing lands for their animals.

The Mongols saw themselves as descended from creatures of the wild. Their first homeland was the Siberian forest, which stretches thousands of miles north, east, and west from the shores of Lake Baikal. The wolf, with its powerful instinct for tracking, pursuing, and killing, provided a symbolic father—dangerous, merciless, and clever—for a people that took their greatest pride in their endurance and hunting ability. But hunting provided a bare means of survival, forcing the Mongols to move constantly to find their prey. For hunters, the life of a steppe nomad represented a better life, a chance to gather herds and trade or raid for weapons and goods.

For this reason, the Mongols moved from the forests to the steppes lying southeast of Lake Baikal. They joined several other nomadic peoples—including the Tatars, Khitan, Jurchen, Merkids, Naimans, Keraits, Unggirats, and Kirghiz—that lived in the hills and plains of the Mongolian Plateau. This land was suitable for grazing, while the Siberian forests to the north still provided game for winter hunting. The Mongols sometimes raided northern China, as did all the steppe peoples, or traded for its weapons and household goods.

But the Mongol homeland remained distant from the well-traveled trade routes to the south. Constant clan and family rivalries also made the steppes a scene of confusion, banditry, and war for dominance and power. The clans plundered each other, raiding camps and taking their captives as household slaves or concubines. Occasionally, a charismatic leader would emerge to unite several clans under his authority—usually in a time of war against neighboring peoples of the steppes. But the Mongols did not have a king, a government, written laws, courts of justice, police, or a standing army. Instead, they had oral customs of law, fought their battles in small bands, paid allegiance to individuals, and settled their differences privately. The Mongols remained a much smaller tribe than the Uighurs, Khitans, Naimans, and Tartars. In the eyes of such stronger and wealthier steppe peoples, the Mongols were disunited, militarily weak, and poor.

To the Chinese, the Mongols were the Mengwu or the Menggu, just one of many uncivilized barbarian tribes from the north. One Chinese chronicler, Li Xinchuan, described them: "The Menggu live to the northwest of the Jurchid; during the Tang dynasty they formed the tribe of the Mengwu. The people are strong and warlike, they can see in the night. They make armour from fish scales in order to protect themselves from stray arrows. . . . They do not cook their food."[2]

The Chinese had experienced Mongol raids for several centuries and could do little to prevent them. The many fortifications, walls, towers, and army garrisons placed in the way of the nomads could not protect every mile of the long frontier. For that reason, politics and diplomacy were used by the Chinese emperors, who constantly sought alliances with the most powerful nomadic leaders. They also plotted with weaker nomadic tribes to rebel against these leaders and keep the tribes in a state of civil war.

The Chinese leaders believed they had little to fear from the Mongols. For the Mongols, the late twelfth century was a time in the wilderness—but also an ideal time for a powerful leader to emerge.

They only needed an individual of great strength, charisma, and vision to unite them. In the early thirteenth-century, they found this individual in Genghis Khan, who transformed the poor, scattered Mongols into conquerors of the largest empire in history.

The Rise of Temuchin

The Mongols found their great leader and unifier in Genghis Khan, born as Temuchin in 1167. He was a member of the Borjigin clan, a group of several hundred families that lived in the Mongol homeland southeast of Lake Baikal, along the River Onon. Temuchin was the son of Ho'elun Ujin and Yesugei, a Borjigin chieftain who named his son after a defeated Tatar enemy. As the son of a chieftain, Temuchin might have had a claim to the leadership of his clan, if not the entire Mongol nation. But Mongol leaders did not inherit their titles. They were elected by their followers and had to achieve power by making helpful alliances and showing leadership in times of war.

Jealousy and the struggle for power made chieftainship hazardous among the Mongols, who were often targets of assassination by their enemies as well as their own followers. When his son was nine years old, Yesugei was poisoned by a group of Tatars, a rival people of the steppes. Temuchin's mother, Ho'elun Ujin, was forced to flee into the valley of the River Onon. There the fatherless family lived in the wild, outcasts who survived on the game they killed and the wild roots and edible plants they foraged.

While still a boy, Temuchin was captured by members of the Tayichi'ud, another Mongol clan, who held him prisoner for several months. He became the personal property of a Tayichi'ud chieftain but was allowed to walk about under the watchful eyes of his captors. One night, when everyone else was sleeping, he escaped from the Tayichi'ud camp and took refuge among the Unggirats people.

While living with the Unggirats, he married Borte, a woman previously engaged to him by his father. Temuchin then became a *nokor* (follower) of Toghrul Khan, a leader of the Keraits (a steppe tribe that later became part of the Mongol confederation) and a former *anda* (a traditional ally and companion) of Temuchin's father Yesugei. The uncertainty of life on the steppes forced young and ambitious men to make alliances such as this, entering the service of a khan (chief) as a *nokor*. These followers lived in the camp of their leaders but were free to leave at any time and serve any khan they liked. For this reason, the successful khan constantly trained his army and sought out battles and raids; his victorious followers won wealth and plunder, the *nokors* remained loyal, and in turn the clan of soldiers attracted new members.

Temuchin's Strategy and Tactics

As a follower of Toghrul Khan, Temuchin was still close to his own boyhood *anda*, Jamukha. Both were skilled warriors and both emerged as the leaders of a small group of Mongol warriors who fought for Toghrul Khan. On several occasions, Temuchin defeated Toghrul's enemies. These victories raised his status among the Mongol tribes and encouraged his own ambitions. In the words of historian David Morgan, "circumstances were propitious for a successful young nomad warrior to build up a following of his own, if he could once make a start.

This is what Temuchin appears to have done. By his audacity, his success in raiding those more powerful than himself, his personal magnetism—whatever it may have been—he began to attract like-minded warriors to his standard."[3] The band of warriors around Temuchin gradually grew into a small army of several hundred men. Temuchin overcame the traditional Mongol lack of cooperation on the battlefield by organizing his men into small, self-sufficient units and training them to fight cohesively. The smaller units were given specific enemy targets and ordered to support other units if needed. Temuchin's leadership and tactics made his unit into one of Toghrul Khan's most effective battalions.

This illustration depicts Temuchin hiding from his Tayichi'ud guards. Temuchin escaped from the Tayichi'ud after several months in captivity.

Toghrul Khan took notice of Temuchin's ability. As a master of the Kerait clan, he needed a man like Temuchin to win a valuable alliance with the emperor of the Qin dynasty in northern China. Eventually the Qin emperor recognized Toghrul Khan as *wang* (king) of the Mongols and employed him as an ally against the powerful Tatars, another steppe people of Mongolia. Temuchin won this campaign for Toghrul Khan by tracking down and defeating a Tatar army in the Khingan Mountains. This battle ended the Tatar threat to the Qin dynasty, while Temuchin took revenge for the poisoning of his father by massacring thousands of Tatar men and families after the battle was decided.

Temuchin's actions inspired fierce loyalty among his officers and fighting men. He was an impressive figure, according to the Persian chronicler Juvaini, who described him as "a man of tall stature, of vigorous build, robust in body, the hair on his face scanty and turned white, with cats' eyes, possessed of dedicated energy, discernment, genius, and understanding, awe-striking, a butcher, just, resolute, an overthrower of enemies, intrepid, sanguinary, and cruel."[4]

A master of battlefield tactics, Temuchin carefully planned in advance every clash with his enemies. Favoring surprise attacks and unexpected formations, he placed his fighters in the best possible position for the battle. When a clan of families and soldiers were faced with battle or the threat of a raid, he organized the entire camp for self-defense. Historian Michael Prawdin describes this preparation:

> The usual practice in such nomadic combats was to make a laager of waggons in the middle of which the flocks and herds were guarded while the warriors descended from the waggons, either to ride against the foe, or to withdraw within the protection of the laager. Temuchin, however, commanded that the carts should be arranged in a circle on one of his extreme wings, and he entrusted the defence of this circle to women and children armed with bows and arrows.[5]

In mock battles, Temuchin trained his armies to outmaneuver enemy units, attack where an attack was not expected, bring overwhelming force, and leave the enemy helpless and ready to surrender. These mock campaigns enforced Temuchin's own ideas of battle tactics and overall strategy. They trained Temuchin's officers and men

Temuchin used mock battles to train his officers and men to cooperate with each other and to obey his orders unquestioningly.

to cooperate with each other and follow the orders of their leader without question. Gradually, Temuchin emerged as Toghrul Khan's most powerful rival for leadership of the Mongols.

Rivalry with Toghrul Khan

Loyalty to Temuchin among his followers grew stronger after the defeat of the Tatars. His success in battle, however, and his leadership ability raised the envy of his patron, Toghrul Khan. In 1204, the khan enlisted Jamukha to defeat the young commander. Although he had pledged lifelong friendship to Temuchin, Jamukha saw a better opportunity in winning this victory for Toghrul Khan. He gathered what remained of the opposition to Temuchin and prepared to fight him.

To face this last threat to his supremacy, Temuchin collected the leaders of his group in a traditional *quriltai*, or meeting, to plan his campaign. He organized his army into small, disciplined groups of tens and hundreds, each unit operating in close cooperation with the others, ready to move instantly on orders brought by messengers, by raised flags, or by a flight of arrows. Familiar with Temuchin's abilities as a commander and facing his large and well-organized force, Jamukha fled the field even before the two armies began their combat. His army was soundly defeated and hundreds of his soldiers put to death. Shortly afterward, Jamukha himself was captured and executed. In 1203, Temuchin also defeated rivals who had gathered under the banner of Toghrul Khan, who was killed during the battle.

After the defeat of Jamukha and Toghrul Khan, his most powerful rivals, Temuchin

assembled another *quriltai* along the Orion River, in what is now northeastern Mongolia, in 1206. To this meeting Temuchin brought his entire family, his companions, his generals, and all the clan leaders of the Mongols, who paid him homage and agreed to serve him in any capacity. He was proclaimed leader of the Mongols and given the title of Genghis Khan (Universal Ruler). The event had religious as well as political significance, as described by biographer Boris Vladimirtsov: "A prominent part at the *Kurultai* of 1206 was played by the sorcerer and shaman Kokchu, son of Munlik, whom the Mongols viewed with superstitious reverence. Kokchu announced that the Everlasting Blue Sky favoured Chingis-Khan who was its own preordained envoy on earth (*jayagatu*) and all his clan."[6]

In the eyes of his followers, Genghis Khan enjoyed the favor of the spirits and of the sky. He embodied the will of these spirits that the Mongols should be a united, powerful nation and that their scattered clans should establish an empire on the steppes. In fact, Genghis Khan had experienced treachery, violence, and the bitter quarrels that divided the tribes of the Mongols. He had lived as an exile, with no friends or allies to rely on, and had melded undisciplined nomads into an effective army. Having gained supreme power, he was now determined to also unite the Mongols into an undivided society, with unquestioning obedience to a single leader.

Universal Ruler

Even before becoming Universal Ruler of the Mongols, Genghis Khan made his commanders swear personal loyalty to him as *nokors*. In return he granted them important commands in the Mongol army. He set up a personal bodyguard, known as a *keshig*, made up of younger relatives of the *nokors*. The members of the *keshig* were personally responsible for the safety of Genghis Khan.

Seeking to lessen the power of the clan chiefs, Genghis Khan promoted them in his own administration, where he could directly control them. As a result of this strategy, the most powerful Mongol leaders owed their careers entirely to him, not to their clan or family origins. But Genghis Khan was also well aware that his leadership would breed jealousy among the most able of his followers. To deal with those who posed any kind of threat to his authority, he exiled them to remote areas or simply found grounds to execute them. Rivalries or feuds—among tribes, within the army, or in the government—were broken up, with all combatants forced to swear personal loyalty to Genghis Khan.

To lay the foundation for a great empire, Genghis also passed down a body of law, orders, and instructions, known as the Great Yasa. The Yasa described how each territory was to be governed, which tasks fell to the governors and administrators, how crimes should be punished, and even how households should be run. The Yasa was dedicated by Genghis Khan with the following passage, as quoted by the Persian historian Rashid al-Din:

> If in the future of 500, 1,000 or 10,000 years, successors who will be born and ascend the throne preserve and do not alter the custom (*yosun*) and the law (*yasa*) of Genghis Khan, which must be applied to [all important events of] the people, Heaven will support their rule. . . . If the great, the military leaders and the emirs of the many descendants of the ruler who will be born in the future, should not adhere strictly to the law, then the power of the state will be shattered and come to an end; no matter how they then seek Genghis Khan, they shall not find him.[7]

Genghis Khan's accomplishments did not end with the unification of the Mongol nation. Nor was he satisfied with victories against scattered armies in the isolated Mongolian steppes. He saw himself as both a great khan and a religious leader, a traditional shaman with a mandate from Tengri, the god of the sky, to march across the world at the head of an army. Under Genghis Khan's leadership, the Mongol people were prepared for a grander task: universal conquest.

The Conquests of Genghis Khan

For the next twenty years, Genghis Khan led the Mongols on an extraordinary campaign of conquest, from China to central Asia, Persia, and as far west as the Caucasus Mountains. He brought a huge domain under his personal control. His goal was to impose Mongol law and administration, collect tribute, and gain the loyalty of the entire world, which would pay homage to his own family as its ruling dynasty.

In his campaigns, Genghis Khan used terror as an effective weapon against his enemies. His reputation as a ruthless killer stemmed from his habit of utterly destroying any city that resisted his armies. But Genghis Khan never made war unnecessarily. The relatively small Mongol army (in

THE BALJUNA COVENANT

In 1203, Temuchin narrowly escaped a plot against his life at the hands of Toghrul Khan, the man to whom he had pledged his loyalty as a *nokor*, or vassal. He then wandered in the wilderness, as he had after the assassination of his father Yesugei. This time, he had command of a small band of nineteen followers. The group rode to the shores of Lake Baljuna in northern Mongolia, where Temuchin planned his campaign of revenge against the khan. In a ceremony that in Mongol tradition marks the founding of Genghis Khan's empire, the men swore an oath of loyalty to Temuchin. This "Baljuna Covenant" became an important event in Mongolian history. Each member of the covenant would be rewarded with a position of authority after the defeat of Toghrul Khan and the *quriltai* of 1206 at which Temuchin was proclaimed Genghis Khan.

In the words of historian Jack Weatherford in *Genghis Khan and the Making of the Modern World*, the Baljuna Covenant represents the essence of the Mongol Empire to be established by Genghis Khan in the coming years:

> The nineteen men with Temujin Khan came from nine different tribes; probably only Temujin and his brother Khasar were actually from the Mongol clans. The others included Merkid, Khitan, and Kereyid. Whereas Temujin was a devout shamanist who worshiped the Eternal Blue Sky and the God Mountain of Burkhan Khaldun, the nineteen included several Christians, three Muslims, and several Buddhists. They were united only in their devotion to Temujin and their oath to him and each other. The oaths sworn at Baljuna created a type of brotherhood, and in transcending kinship, ethnicity, and religion, it came close to being a type of modern civic citizenship based upon personal choice and commitment. This connection became a metaphor for the new type of community among Temujin's followers that would eventually dominate as the basis of unity within the Mongol Empire.

comparison to more established states like China) could not afford large losses in battle. Genghis Khan used its fast maneuvering ability to outflank enemies and convince them to surrender as quickly as possible. He also was an expert politician who gained allies by overthrowing tyrants and playing one enemy against another.

In 1215, after a campaign of many years, Genghis Khan's army conquered Zhengdu, the capital of the Qin empire. The Universal Ruler next turned to Kara-Khitai, a steppe empire lying west of Mongolia, which was ruled by a Naiman tribesman, Kuchlug. Although he was also a man of the steppes and a great khan in his own right, Kuchlug had overthrown the previous ruler in a coup. This act of treachery, and his religious intolerance and persecution of Muslims (Kuchlug himself was a Buddhist),

This fifteenth-century Iranian illustration depicts Genghis Khan's army subduing the Kara-Khitai.

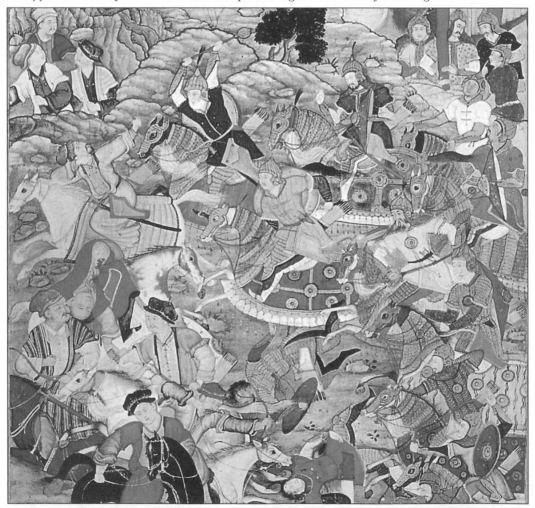

TATARS AND MONGOLS

Since the Middle Ages, several names have been given to Genghis Khan's people: Mongols, Tatars, and Tartars. In the twelfth century, the Tatars were a powerful tribe from eastern Mongolia, who dominated the deserts and steppes north of China. They were allied with the Qin dynasty of northern China and rivals of the other powerful tribes of the steppes: Keraits, Merkids, Unggirats, Naimans, and the tribe of Genghis Khan.

Genghis Khan defeated and destroyed the Tatars before his acceptance by all the steppe tribes as their "universal ruler." In Russia and Europe, however, the name "Tatars" was adopted to designate the people of Mongolia who were loyal to Genghis Khan (the name was also spelled "Tartar"—signifying for many the origins of these people in Tartarus, a traditional Greek name for the Christian hell). Genghis Khan's given name was Temuchin—the name of a Tatar tribesman whom Temuchin's own father had killed. When the Tatars avenged this death by poisoning Genghis Khan's father, Temuchin made it his lifelong goal to avenge the killing. His defeat of the Tatars eliminated them as a distinct Mongolian tribe—although their name endured in Europe for centuries.

made him extremely unpopular among his own people. Kuchlug was easily defeated by Genghis Khan's general Jebei Noyon in 1218, after which he was hunted down and killed. After this victory, many Khitans entered the service of Genghis Khan, who adopted many of the administrative structures and practices of Kara-Khitai to build his own empire.

In the west, in 1218, the treachery of an Arab governor inspired the next great conquest of Genghis Khan in Khwarezm, a sultanate (kingdom) covering the deserts and plains of Central Asia. The ancient Silk Road linked the steppes of Mongolia with the cities of Khwarezm and its capital of Samarkand, the wealthiest city in central Asia. The two regions were closely tied by this trade, and Genghis Khan made a treaty of peace and friendship with Khwarezm soon after becoming Universal Ruler of the Mongols. But the good relations ended when a Mongol caravan was placed under arrest by Inalchik (or Inal-khan), the governor of the Khwarezm city of Utrar. After questioning four Mongol merchants who owned the caravan, Inalchik accused them of spying and put them to death.

Genghis Khan would not tolerate disloyalty and treachery, especially from a man he had no quarrel with. By this time, he was also confident of his ability to punish any

EUROPE ENCOUNTERS THE MONGOLS

Early thirteenth-century Europe had no knowledge of the Mongols and very little of east Asia. The distant countries at the other end of the Silk Road had never been visited by a westerner, and no European ship had even sailed beyond the coasts of Arabia or as far as the Indian Ocean.

Word of the campaigns of Genghis Khan reached Europe via the Crusaders, Christian knights who held small feudal states in the Middle East. Thirteen years after Genghis Khan's death in 1227 Mongol armies invaded Europe, ravaging Poland and Hungary. Travelers and ambassadors began heading east to investigate the Mongols. Matthew Paris was an English historian who described the Mongol onslaught on Europe and gave a fanciful account of Mongol history and customs.

John of Plano Carpini was a traveler sent to Mongolia by Pope Innocent IV, the head of the Catholic Church, after the Mongol invasion of Europe in 1240. Carpini and his companion Benedict traveled to Mongolia by walking and riding across the plains of southern Russia and the deserts of central Asia. They visited the camp of Guyuk, a grandson of Genghis Khan who was the third great khan of the Mongols from 1246 until his death in 1248, where they were given courteous treatment. The khan received the European ambassadors and gave them a letter demanding the homage of the pope and all of Europe to the Mongol ruler. Carpini wrote a report in 1247 known as the *Historia Mongalorum*, in which he describes Mongol customs as well as the Mongol army.

In 1253 William of Rubruck, a priest and missionary, was sent by King Louis IX of France to the court of the Mongols, where he met with Mongke, Guyuk's successor as Great Khan, at the Mongol capital of Karakorum. Mongke invited William to participate in a debate on the virtues of Christianity, Islam, and Buddhism, held for the entertainment and enlightenment of the khan. This famous debate and his encounter with the Mongols are described in William's *Itinerarium*.

The most famous European visitor, Marco Polo, was an Italian merchant who spent twenty years in the Far East. From 1275 until 1292 he lived and worked in Khanbalik, the capital of the Mongol empire in northern China. Part of this time was spent at the court of Kublai Khan, the Mongol ruler of China. After returning to Europe, he wrote *The Travels*, an account of his journey and of the customs of many people of Asia, with special interest in the history and administration of China under Kublai Khan.

bad behavior among his own vassals as well as distant allies. He sent ambassadors to Mohammed Shah, the ruler of Khwarezm, with a warning of what would happen next:

> You have, by signing our accord, pledged yourself to protect the merchants and not to harm them; but you have acted faithlessly and broken your word. Disloyalty is disgraceful, especially disgraceful in the case of a sultan of Islam. If, however, you maintain that Inal-khan's deed was not carried out at your behest, then hand Inal-khan over to me so that we may punish him for his crime, thus reassuring the masses and preventing the spilling of blood. Otherwise, it is war.[8]

When Mohammed Shah received Genghis Khan's threat, he ordered Inalchik to put some of the Mongol ambassadors to death and send the rest back with their heads shaved (in many Asian societies, a humiliating insult). An outraged Genghis Khan assembled an enormous army of 200,000, which included a battalion of siege towers and Chinese cannons that had been used against the cities of the Qin empire. The khan then ordered the invasion and destruction of Khwarezm.

The Mongols first defeated Utrar, where Inalchik was captured and put to death in the most gruesomely painful manner the Mongols could devise—by having molten metal poured into his eyes. After Utrar, the Mongols defeated the cities of Bukhara, Otrar, and Samarkand, Mohammed Shah's capital. Protected by a garrison of 100,000 ill-equipped soldiers, Samarkand surren-

dered after only five days. The Mongols put all the armed defenders to death, chased the inhabitants from the city, and razed the city's walls, monuments, palaces, markets, and homes. Once the wealthiest city on the Silk Road, Samarkand was reduced to uninhabitable ruins, while Mohammed Shah fled to an island in the Caspian Sea, where he died of natural causes in 1220.

These conquests and massacres in Khwarezm gave Genghis Khan a bad reputation that has stayed with him for centuries. In the view of many historians, the Mongols of the thirteenth century were indiscriminate killers whose sole interest was plunder and conquest. In fact, Genghis Khan spared as many cities as he destroyed, and he destroyed cities only as an example for those others determined to resist him. His main interest lay in building a worldwide Mongol empire that would last. In Genghis Khan's opinion, the life of a Mongol nomad represented an ideal to which the entire world, under his rule, should aspire.

This nomadic life of the steppes had given the Mongols finely honed skills in hunting, raiding, and plundering and had also prepared them for long campaigns in distant lands. It took the strong-willed and charismatic Genghis Khan to unite the feuding Mongol clans and to instill the discipline needed for world conquest. The key to this conquest was the Mongol army, which consisted of mounted archers who struck with lightning speed and relied on surprise and carefully coordinated maneuvers to win its battles. The training and organization of this army, under Genghis Khan's direction, made it one of the most effective fighting forces in history.

CHAPTER TWO

AN UNSTOPPABLE FORCE: THE MONGOL ARMY

Across China, central Asia, and Persia, the news of the Mongol conquests arrived well in advance of Genghis Khan's armies. At first, there was no concern—only contempt. Genghis Khan was unknown, and in the eyes of outsiders, the steppe tribes were poor, weak, and uncivilized. The Mongols seemed to pose no more of a threat than other such nomads, who had always been defeated or assimilated outside the borders of their own country.

Before Genghis Khan's time, the Mongols had no regular army. Instead, when needed, the tribes and clans formed temporary confederations. The khans, elected by their peers for their courage, assembled these confederations for war against their rivals, then broke them up when the fighting was finished. The stronger the leader, the longer the confederation could be held together. If a khan grew weak or began to suffer defeat on the battlefield, he would be quickly abandoned by his followers.

It was not until Genghis Khan's time that a Mongol army—superbly trained and equipped—marched out of the steppes of Mongolia for the purpose of foreign conquest. From a nation of nomads and hunters, divided into feuding clans and families, Genghis Khan created a disciplined military,

the best in the world in the medieval age. To everyone who encountered it, this army brought terror and defeat. For decades, the Mongols won every battle they fought, due to Genghis Khan's ability to organize and lead his soldiers and officers.

Mongol Weaponry

The Mongols relied on several key weapons to fight their battles. These included the long and short composite bows, which were capable of firing an arrow or heavy bolt (made of a single piece of wood) up to 300 yards (274m). The arrowheads were made of iron, shaped to either pierce armor or to flay the flesh of enemies. Mongol soldiers were trained to shoot in all directions, forward and backward, while ducking behind the heads or under the bellies of their horses and even while galloping at full speed away from the enemy. The Mongols also carried battle-axes and short, curved iron swords known as scimitars. These weapons were ideal for slashing an enemy combatant in a close-in fight. Their lances were long poles with sharpened tips, used for charging or for throwing at a group of enemy soldiers.

For protection, the Mongols wore steel or leather helmets, neck coverings made of leather, and body armor of hard leather,

Skilled at fighting on horseback, Mongol warriors used composite bows to shoot iron-tipped arrows at their enemies in battle.

sometimes covered with metal scales (the leather was boiled and then coated with a resin that made it tough and durable). Their undershirts, made of dense raw silk, protected them by wrapping around any arrowhead that entered the body, which helped to prevent infection. Mongol soldiers also carried small round shields made of willow frames and covered with stretched hide.

These weapons were ideal for fighting in small groups against mounted, lightly equipped enemies. But Mongol tactics and weaponry changed when Genghis Khan led his larger, well-organized armies against cities protected by high stone walls. From the Chinese, the Mongols captured or bought useful siege engines, such as siege towers and catapults, to hurl boulders and flaming objects into a city.

The Mongols were skilled horsemen who were able to mock pursuing armies by riding their horses in unusual positions.

They used bronze cannons, first developed by the Chinese, to hurl iron balls against fortifications. Their sappers, whose job was to destroy enemy defenses, dug tunnels in order to plant explosive devices under city walls.

An Army of Horsemen

All Mongol men, from the time they could pick up a bow or sword and fight, were considered members of the army, unless their occupations (such as priest or doctor) were more useful to the nation. And since childhood, all had spent much of their time in the saddle. Although they grew skilled in the use of artillery and siege weapons, the Mongols remained an army of cavalry, with no foot soldiers. They could endure several days and nights on the back of a horse, sleeping, eating, hunting, and, most important, fighting. According to one contemporary source,

They ride fast bound unto their horses, which are not very great in stature, but exceedingly strong, and maintained with little provender [food]. They . . . fight constantly and valiantly with javelins, maces, battle-axes and swords. But specially they are excellent archers, and cunning warriors with their bows. Their backs are slightly armed, that they may not flee. They withdraw not themselves from the combat till they see the chief standard of their General give back. Vanquished, they ask no favor, and vanquishing, they show no compassion.[9]

The ability to move rapidly across long distances was the foundation of the battle strategy developed by Genghis Khan. His men could ride 80 or even 100 miles (128 or 160km) in a single day, and because the Mongols had no infantry, their units could move much faster than an ordinary army and take their enemies completely by surprise. Mongol soldiers prepared for these journeys by bringing several horses. This allowed them to change mounts and regularly rest their animals, or replace a horse if it was killed in battle.

The Mongol Order of Battle

To the feuding Mongols, Genghis Khan introduced two vital elements: organization and discipline. He also instilled a strong sense of loyalty among the Mongols to their comrades-in-arms. Before the time of Genghis Khan, peacetime had always meant trouble for the Mongols, who turned their skill as fighters and horsemen against each other in the endless quest for good grazing and pasture lands. In Genghis Khan's army, Mongol soldiers were sworn to fight and if necessary die for each other, to stand guard at all times, and to share weapons, food, and sleeping quarters.

Under Genghis Khan, the Mongol army numbered between 100,000 and 200,000 men. This force was divided into *tumens* of 10,000, *minghans* of 1,000, *jaguns* of 100, and *arbans* of 10. The members of an *arban* always lived, rode, and fought together. They were sworn to defend each other at all costs and to give up their lives with honor.

REMEMBERING THE MONGOLS IN POLAND

The people of Kraków, Poland, have not forgotten the Mongol siege of their city, which took place nearly eight centuries ago in 1241. Before the arrival of the Mongol horde, the medieval defenders of Kraków shut the gates and lined the high walls with armed defenders. A watchman was posted on one of the towers of the cathedral, the highest place in the city. A trumpeter was to begin playing the *hejnal*, a warning signal, when the assault began.

After a few days, the Mongols approached the city walls. From atop the cathedral, which towered high over the city's main square, the frantic trumpeter repeated the *hejnal*, as the people of Kraków prepared themselves for battle. Suddenly, the music stopped. Those scattered below in the square looked up at the tower. A Mongol arrow, fired from hundreds of yards away, had pierced the trumpeter's throat, ending his life. To this day, from the same place atop the market square of Kraków, the tune is sounded every hour to commemorate the assault of the Mongols and the brave but failed defense of the city.

By tradition, the eldest man of the group was the commander, but the other members could elect an alternative leader if they wished. The leaders of the *jaguns* were also elected, while the commanders of *tumens* and *minghans* were selected by Genghis Khan himself for their ability and personal loyalty. In order to prevent clan rivalries from weakening his army, he scattered members of a single clan to different units and did not permit any man to change or to leave his unit.

Genghis Khan also organized a powerful *keshig*, an elite corps of 10,000 men entrusted with his personal safety. The *keshig* included divisions of a day guard (*turgaut*), a night guard (*kebteut*), and arrow-bearers (*korchi*), each numbering 1,000 men. Genghis Khan personally selected recruits for the *keshig* from the ranks of ordinary soldiers in the army. Many were the sons and younger relatives of Genghis Khan's advisers, aides, and generals. They were responsible for guarding the khan, for watching over his camp, for protecting weapons and banners, and for supervising the khan's *ordo*, his household and servants. They also provided a reserve of trained young men for important military posts. Mainly though, they accompanied the khan into battle and

This scene from a modern film about Genghis Khan depicts the warriors of the keshig, Genghis Khan's *elite fighting force.*

were used as an overwhelming attacking force at the decisive moment of the fight. As quoted by historian Boris Vladimirtsov, Genghis Khan describes how he selected members of the *keshig* from the Mongol elite: "Now that the Sky has ordered me to govern all nations, let there be recruited from the myriads, thousands and hundreds, ten thousand men, archers and others, to be my personal guard (*keshig*). These men, who will be attached to my person, must be chosen from among the sons of nobles or of free men (*tarkat*) and must be agile, well-built and hardy."[10]

The *keshig* was the aristocracy of the military, used by Genghis Khan to recruit the future generals of his army. "You are the body-guardsmen of the night watch . . . for the peace of my body and soul," he told them; "you mounted guards all round my tent, on rainy and snowy nights, as well as on the clear nights of alarms and of battles with the enemy. . . . My descendants shall regard these body-guardsmen as a monument of myself, and take great care of them; they shall not excite their resentment, and shall regard them as good genii [spirits]."[11]

The *keshig* and all other members of the Mongol army went through constant training, maneuvers, mock battles, and target practice. The respect and reverence of his people allowed Genghis Khan to impose this heavy training as well as a very tough discipline. His orders and his battle tactics were unquestioned, although he allowed his best generals liberty to fight and move their units as they saw fit. The rest of the army, like the Mongol people in general, accepted the many rules he imposed on every aspect of their lives or suffered death or exile as their punishment.

Discipline in the Mongol Army

Under the command of Genghis Khan's hand-picked generals, the army drilled itself with hunting parties on the open steppes. The *tumens* formed a large circle, as wide as 50 miles (80km) across, and converged over the course of several days, driving any game they had surrounded toward the center. Hunting instilled the virtues of patience, coordination, and discipline—a very important quality in any army, but particularly among the Mongols. According to historian Timothy May:

> By the thirteenth century, nomad horse archer armies already possessed a long history of success. Yet, the one which Chinggis Khan created perfected this form. He added the essential element that separated the Mongols from their peers: discipline. This enabled him to overcome the assortment of tribal confederations and alliances, which he faced before becoming the ruler of all Mongolia. While other armies would disintegrate in order to loot the dead and baggage of an enemy in flight, Chinggis Khan ordered his armies to wait until victory was complete. Those who disobeyed this command would be struck down.[12]

Displaying cowardice, retreating from battle, or leaving one's post without permission were punished by death. The unit commanders made a daily examination of equipment; if a soldier lacked anything he was supposed to have, he was whipped or beaten. Genghis Khan himself ordered and carried out many of these punishments.

If he heard of an offense committed by someone who was not in his presence, he would send a messenger to carry out the sentence in his name. A Mongol general faced by a humble messenger from the khan had to prostrate himself on the ground. He had to hear out the messenger and, if ordered, submit to any punishment the messenger was to carry out—including execution.

Genghis Khan also laid down a strict ban on looting during battle. Before his time, the Mongols had fought as a mob, with each man seeking only to gain for himself what he could take from the home of a defeated enemy. The instinct for raiding was strong, but as a result, Mongol armies had often deteriorated into disorganized bands of thieves. To prevent this, Genghis Khan ordered no looting of homes or cities until a complete victory was won over the enemy. In addition, he decreed that a dead soldier's fair share of goods won in battle must be turned over to his widow and family. This measure prevented quarrels over property within the army and enhanced the loyalty of his followers, who knew that their own deaths would not leave their families destitute.

Battle Tactics

Under such leadership and discipline, the Mongol armies prepared well for their campaigns. The offices sent spies against the enemy to learn the size and position of its armies, the morale of its citizens, and the strength of its defenses. Mongol generals had specific goals and timetables, with each *tumen* given a particular task. The army usually rode in columns, with two wings flanking a powerful, central force. Small companies of scouts—ten or just a handful

of men—were sent well ahead of the main force. The scouts used signal fires, whistling arrows, and flags to show the movement and location of enemy forces.

The ten-thousand-strong *tumens* of the Mongol army were fast-moving as well as self-sufficient. They could live off the land and, if necessary, from the large herds of horses that accompanied them. There were two kinds of *tumens*: heavy cavalry, used for close combat, and light cavalry, which moved more quickly and relied on the bow and arrow. Each *tumen* had small companies of engineers, who built siege weapons on the way from available timber. The *tumens* moved with a very light supply train, often traveling during the coldest winter months. The winter allowed them the element of surprise—no enemy expected or wanted to fight in the cold and snow. Winter also lessened the need for water and provided better hunting.

This organization allowed Genghis Khan and his generals to move their compact units around a battlefield easily and take quick advantage of the enemy's weaknesses. It was common for Mongol leaders to divide their army, allowing the *tumens* to disperse across the countryside and converge at the last moment on the enemy. This enabled the Mongols to surprise and outflank their enemies and also had the effect of making any Mongol army appear much larger than it really was.

Once the battle began, the most common strategy was for skirmishers to advance, engage, and disrupt the enemy's front lines. The long-distance archers then fired into the enemy lines from several directions. The barrage confused opponents who often could not tell where, exactly, the main assault was coming from. After this hail of arrows, the Mongols mounted a headlong charge of heavy cavalry. Against an aggressive or much larger enemy force, a common tactic was to retreat and tempt the enemy into pursuit. The archers then unleashed another salvo of arrows before the Mongol horsemen turned and charged.

Often outnumbered, the Mongols relied on patience, caution, and tactics of deception to defeat their enemies. They attacked when unexpected—often before dawn or as sunset was approaching. At the command of their leaders, they could assume any one of several different formations, depending on how the enemy had arranged its units. When facing a long front, the Mongols brought up their archers in waves. Each wave fired and then quickly moved to the back, allowing the next wave to advance and fire. In this way, the Mongols kept up a continuous attack on the front ranks of the enemy, who found themselves under a constant, deadly rain of iron-tipped arrows. When vastly outnumbered and unwilling to give battle, the Mongols used the cover of night to divide into scattered groups of ten. These *arbans* would hit and run from many directions and then retreat before the enemy had a chance to organize a counterattack.

A tumen was a Mongol fighting force of ten thousand men. As shown in this film reenactment, these units could quickly surround an enemy on the battlefield.

THE BANNER OF GENGHIS KHAN

Mongol warriors of all ranks carried their soul and fighting spirit in a banner known as a *sulde*. The *sulde* was a spear or lance decorated with strands of hair from the owner's best fighting horses. The hair was thought to channel the natural forces of sunlight and wind to the owner. In turn, the *sulde* absorbed the spirit of the owner with the passing of years. The *sulde* was a guardian totem and a symbol of its owner's fighting ability. By custom, it was planted just outside the owner's tent to identify him.

Genghis Khan had two banners, a white one for his home in Mongolia, where he lived in peace, and a black banner that he used while on campaign. Although the white banner disappeared after his death, Genghis Khan's black banner was preserved as a sacred relic for more than seven hundred years in the Shankh Monastery, in central Mongolia. There it was carefully guarded by Buddhist monks. The banner disappeared during the 1930s, when Mongolia came under the domination of the Soviet Union and the monastery was sacked by the Soviet army. Since then, the missing black *sulde* of Genghis Khan has remained a powerful symbol of the empire and nation he founded.

Genghis Khan's tactics proved superior to the customary battlefield maneuvers of medieval times, when armies, mostly made up of heavily armed foot soldiers, fought in slow-moving masses. The British historian B.H. Liddell Hart put Genghis Khan and his leading general, Subedei, in the first chapter of his book *Great Captains Unveiled*, concluding the following about the Mongol military machine:

they proved that mobility is the king-pin of tactics, as of strategy; that lightly armed troops can beat more heavily armed ones if their mobility is sufficiently superior . . . the Mongols solved the ever-difficult problem of co-operation between arms which have radically different qualities and limitations. The single arm they used [cavalry] was that which possessed the highest degree of mobility, and in this lay the secret of their unbroken run of victory.[13]

The Use of Massacre

Genghis Khan also developed an effective method of overcoming fortified cities—propaganda. Any city unwise enough to resist was doomed to a massacre when it finally fell. It was standard practice to level these cities and slaughter their inhabitants—soldiers and civilians, men and women, children and animals. (The Mongols had no respect for townspeople, who in their eyes lived a soft, useless life. The only prisoners the Mongols took were scholars or artisans whose knowledge might prove useful, able-bodied men to serve in their army as slaves, and concubines.) However, a few people were allowed to escape with their lives. Their task was to spread the news of Mongol atrocities to the next town, encouraging a quick surrender.

The wholesale slaughter of the population of any city daring to resist the Mongol army had an important purpose: It was the Mongol way of persuading enemies to surrender without a fight. During Genghis Khan's early campaigns in central Asia, many cities defied his armies and paid a very severe price. In large areas of central Asia, this practice had a permanent effect. The northeastern region of what is now Iran, a place known as Khorasan, was completely laid waste by the Mongols and remains a poor, desolate region in modern times, nearly eight centuries after Genghis Khan's army arrived. After the destruction of Khorasan, the Mongols found that cities farther west were quite ready and willing to surrender to them.

The threat of these Mongol massacres inspired paralyzing terror. According to the Arab historian Ibn al-Athir, "Stories have been related to me . . . which the hearer can scarcely credit, as to the terror of them. . . . And I have heard that one of them [a Mongol soldier] took a man captive, but had not with him any weapon wherewith to kill him; and he said to his prisoner, 'Lay your head on the ground and do not move'; and he did

so, and the [Mongol] went and fetched his sword and slew him therewith."[14]

Genghis Khan saw rumor and fear as vital weapons in his arsenal. The first society to experience this great fear was China, an ancient, wealthy civilization lying south of Mongolia. For centuries, Chinese leaders had effectively dealt with the Mongols and the other tribes by playing off one leader against another. The Chinese had also built a long string of defensive walls, fortresses, and look-out towers on their northern frontier to slow the nomad raids.

These strategies worked well—until the time of Genghis Khan. The first task he set himself after his election in 1206 was the conquest of the Qin dynasty of northern China. Genghis Khan's creation—the near-invincible army of the Mongols—would ensure this conquest and that of half the world over the next two decades.

The Defeat of the Qin

In Genghis Khan's own view, his most important victory was the conquest of the Qin dynasty. To the steppe tribes, the Chinese had always been contemptible farmers and laborers—a tempting source of loot. China and the nomads had been enemies for centuries; war, raiding, and banditry were common along their frontiers. But Chinese emperors had always managed to keep the nomads at bay. In the words of historian David Morgan, "There was a standard imperial Chinese policy for dealing with them. They would be carefully watched, and if one nomadic chief seemed to be gaining power and influence at the expense of others, Chinese subsidies, recognition and titles would be offered to one of his rivals, who would be encouraged to cut the upstart down to size."[15]

Genghis Khan leads an assault on the city of Zhongdu in 1214. Although the city was well fortified, it fell to the invaders after a year-long siege.

To the Mongols of Genghis Khan's time, China meant enormous riches, vast grazing lands, control of wealthy cities and new trade routes, and a vital base for the waging of war on the Song dynasty of southern China. By 1213, Genghis Khan had conquered the lands of the Qin as far south as the Great Wall (which did very little to hinder his campaign). In 1214 the Mongols began the assault on the capital city of Zhongdu, a city protected by nine hundred towers, three wide moats, and thirteen fortified gates. Believing his domain safe behind these high, strong walls and moats, the Qin emperor refused to come out of the city to give battle. Although he had a much larger army, most of his men fought on foot, and he knew that no army of infantry could match the skill and ruthlessness of the tough Mongol horsemen from the north.

But it was not a cavalry charge that defeated Zhongdu. Always ready to adapt their tactics to the situation at hand, the Mongols began by cutting off food and reinforcements. Catapults hurled huge stones against the walls and doors, gradually reducing them to heaps of dusty rubble. Sappers—experts at destruction of walls, towers, and other defenses—dug underneath the walls to undermine their foundations, and burning arrows were shot into the city to sow confusion and fear.

After a siege lasting a year, the Mongols breached the 40-foot (12m) walls of the city. The people of Zhongdu prepared for the worst, knowing that, because they had dared to defend themselves, the Mongols would not spare any of them. The Qin emperor realized that further resistance was futile and that, if he should fall into Mongol hands, his own life would not be spared. He fled for the city of Kaifeng, on the Yellow River far to the south, leaving Zhongdu to its fate. The gates of the city opened, and during the next several days the Mongols looted the city and killed thousands of its inhabitants.

Genghis Khan defeated several more cities and left much of northern China a wasteland. Millions of people died as a result of his campaigns, and millions more were left without homes, farms, or property.

GENGHIS KHAN'S CAT AND BIRD TRICK

In addition to siege engines and deadly arrow storms, the Mongols used several sly tricks to overcome city defenses. According to one legend, Genghis Khan once sent a message to the ruler of a Qin city, offering to retreat if he was given a tribute of a thousand cats and ten thousand birds. When the ransom was paid, the khan ordered flaming cloth tied to the tails of the birds and cats and then released them into the city, setting it ablaze.

The estates of the north were turned into hunting parks for the Mongol horsemen, while the khan considered simply converting northern China into an empty grassland, suitable only for grazing sheep and horses. For the Chinese, the Mongols were a disaster, bringing only death, hardship, and humiliation. A generation after Genghis Khan's death, his grandson Kublai Khan would impose a Mongol ruling dynasty on the Chinese that would endure for a century. To the Chinese, the unthinkable had occurred: tyranny by unwashed and unprincipled barbarians.

Genghis Khan and the Mongols did not see it the same way. To them, the Mongol life was the ideal life, and Mongol society was in harmony with the natural world and the world of the spirits. Although outsiders saw them as lawless raiders, the Mongols had an elaborate code of conduct among themselves and an intricate system of family relationships that helped them survive in their very harsh surroundings.

CHAPTER THREE

THE CODE OF THE MONGOLS

The Mongol Empire was the creation of Genghis Khan, whose goal was to establish a universal Mongol realm. For the Great Khan and his followers, the life of the steppes could not be improved on, and after the rise of the Mongol Empire, the Mongols remained as they had always been, nomads and hunters unwilling to accept a settled life. Yet Genghis Khan did not refuse to adopt certain benefits of civilization. He adapted Mongol traditions in order to break the old clan system and to create laws and an administration suitable for a great empire. According to historian Paul Ratchnevsky,

He grasped the importance of writing and, after the defeat of the Naimans [a rival steppe tribe], had the Mongol princes instructed in the Uighur script. . . . Genghis expressed his pleasure at the humanistic teaching of the Uighur Yelian Temur; he valued the medical expertise of the Iranians and had an eye infection treated by a Persian doctor; craftsmen were spared and scribes attained high positions.[16]

Genghis Khan's own people lacked the experience to govern. The Mongol clans

obeyed their chieftains and lived independently of the other clans. They knew little about politics, elections, administration, and law "With an able warrior to lead them," in the words of the English historian J.J. Saunders, "it was no great task to subdue other nomadic or semi-nomadic tribes . . . but how could an illiterate, barbarous people conquer and hold ancient civilized states? . . . His own Mongols could not help him: hence he enlisted the services of advisers and officials from more advanced societies."[17]

With the help of these foreign advisers, Genghis Khan set down a new code of law and an administration to govern the Mongol Empire. This code was patterned after the ideas and goals of Genghis Khan himself. It was based on his experience in leading small bands of warriors from one end of the steppes to the other. The code of Genghis Khan helped to unify the Mongols, serving as the basis of law in future Mongol dynasties in China, central Asia, and Persia.

The Great Yasa

Until the time of Genghis Khan, the Mongols had no written language or code of laws. They lived according to customs and taboos passed on from one generation to the next.

One such tradition was the ban on marriage between members of the same clan. Another concerned the ritual slaughter of animals, which was always done outside the home. The spilling of blood indoors was taboo among the Mongols, who saw their homes as shelter from the forces of nature and from any form of violence.

There were no courts, judges, or prisons on the steppes of Mongolia. When crimes such as murder, kidnapping, and theft were committed, individual victims or their family had to seek justice on their own. Vengeance for wrongdoing was an affair carried out in private. Men who made enemies dealt with them personally, and Genghis Khan himself often followed this custom. Early in his reign, a powerful shaman named Teb Tenggri attempted to estrange the khan from his brothers in an effort to gain more authority for himself. Genghis Khan settled the matter in the traditional way. Teb Tenggri was invited to the khan's tent, where he was met by his most bitter rival, Genghis Khan's younger brother Temuge. As Genghis Khan looked on, Temuge and several companions wrestled the shaman to the ground outside the tent, broke his spine, and left him there, paralyzed, to die of hunger and thirst.

During Genghis Khan's reign as Universal Ruler, he established a new body of law, orders, and instructions, known as the Great Yasa. In the Mongolian language, *yasa* means "rule," "order," or "decree." The Great Yasa contained the khan's orders as well as state secrets to be known only to him and his close advisers and family members. According to tradition the Yasa was recorded on scrolls, in the Uighur script that Genghis Khan had adopted, and kept locked away in the khan's palace complex.

Eventually the Yasa in its original form disappeared, although some historians doubt that a physical copy ever existed. The code survives only in secondhand accounts of chroniclers from Persia, China, and Europe.

The code applied to all the Mongol tribes. It described the government of each territory, the tasks of the governors and administrators, the punishment for crimes, even the running of households. The individual decrees, known as *bilik*, originated in judgments and pronouncements made by Genghis Khan himself.

The Yasa imposed the death penalty for a wide variety of crimes, reflecting a harsh and demanding environment. Death was the penalty for lying and for making a false accusation. Death was also imposed for stealing and even for breaking the taboo against relieving oneself in a stream or inside a house. For adultery among members of a tribe, the punishment was also death—but adultery with a foreigner was tolerated. To avoid this punishment, it was common for Mongol men to challenge and kill husbands before seizing their wives for themselves.

Crimes of theft were usually punished by death, but horse stealing was punished by requiring the thief to return the missing horse and nine more to the victim. If the thief did not possess nine horses, he had to surrender his own children; if he had no children, he was to be put to death. Anyone finding stolen property had to seek out the owner and return the property in full; if the finder failed to do this, he was considered a thief and subject to execution.

The theft of people—kidnapping wives and children—had long plagued Mongol society. This had caused many blood feuds and also made the legitimacy of children,

This thirteenth-century illustration depicts Mongols preparing to ritually slaughter their horses as a sacrifice to their gods.

and their right to inherit property, a constant source of fighting and tension. To deal with this problem, Genghis Khan declared all children to be legitimate and entitled to inherit property, whether they were the children of first wives, lesser wives, or concubines.

Rules of Private Life

The Great Yasa reached deep into the conduct of everyday life and into the Mongol household. One of the most important decrees Genghis Khan ever passed, for example, forbade his people from taking another Mongol captive as a household slave. The condition of slavery forced an individual's loyalty to a single family or clan, rather than to the nation, and such a condition was no longer to be tolerated. Only foreign captives could become slaves.

Other rules prohibited the washing of clothes and bathing or washing one's hands in running water in the spring or summer, a practice that the Mongols believed caused thunderstorms. Rules on hospitality and the sharing of food were even stricter. It was forbidden to eat in the presence of others without sharing food, and it was forbidden to eat the food offered by a stranger unless the stranger tasted it first (a guard against poisoning). The Mongols were directed to eat no more than others at a single meal, and no one could step over a campfire used for cooking or a plate or dish used for eating. Hands were considered unclean, and anyone drinking water had to use a cup or other vessel—not the hands—to draw it. The Yasa also guided the use of alcohol, suggesting drinking at the most three times a month.

WILLIAM OF RUBRUCK VISITS THE MONGOLS

William of Rubruck, a Franciscan monk who accompanied the French king Louis IX to the Middle East in 1248, was the first European to visit the Mongol capital at Karakorum, in what is now central Mongolia. In a memoir translated by British scholar W.W. Rockhill, he describes the Mongol capital and the traditional Mongol system of justice:

> As to their justice you must know that when two men fight together no one dares interfere, even a father dare not aid a son; but he who has the worse of it may appeal to the court of the lord, and if anyone touches him after the appeal, he is put to death. . . . They inflict capital punishment on no one unless he be taken in the act or confesses. When one is accused by a number of persons, they torture him so that he confesses. They punish homicide with capital punishment, and also co-habiting with a woman not one's own. By not one's own, [I] mean not his wife or bondwoman, for with one's slaves one may do as one pleases. They also punish with death grand larceny, but as for petty thefts, such as that of a sheep, so long as one has not repeatedly been taken in the act, they beat him cruelly, and if they administer a hundred blows they must use a hundred sticks: I speak of the case of those beaten under order of authority. In like manner false envoys, that is to say persons who pass themselves off as ambassadors but who are not, are put to death. Likewise sorcerers . . . for such they consider to be witches.

Genghis Khan watches as a blindfolded criminal is brutally whipped.

As hunting was still the most important means of getting food, many decrees of the Yasa related to this task. The Yasa limited the hunting season to the months between October and March. Animals were protected during the spring and summer months, when they normally gave birth. The code also set down very specific means of slaughtering animals for food—according to one decree, the animal had to have its chest opened and its heart squeezed by hand until it died.

The Khan's Obedient Society

Mongol men and women were responsible for following the decrees of Genghis Khan and for assuring the obedience of other family members. Likewise, each member of a ten-man *arban*, or army squad, upheld the obedience of the others and was liable for violations by any member of the group. Mongol civilians and soldiers lived not as individuals but as members of a close-knit community, in which a person's needs and wants were subordinate to the collective welfare of the nation.

Although his decrees were imposed and obeyed from the time of his accession as Universal Ruler in 1206, Genghis Khan formally proclaimed the new law code at a *quriltai* of 1219. This *quriltai* was, in effect, an acclamation of the new order imposed by the Universal Ruler. Many historians look on this event as the founding of Mongolia and the Yasa as Genghis Khan's single greatest achievement. "The great khan sought to mark the affirmation of his power by an event that would establish a new era," comments Michael Hoang. "The *jasa*, being a tangible manifestation of his prestige, served to confirm his legitimacy. Having brought more than twenty peoples to their knees in

the name of his righteousness, the law giver now wished to justify his actions."[18]

Traditional Mongol society had thwarted the ambitions of Genghis Khan many times in his life. As Temuchin, the son of an outcast family, he had no titles or prestige of his own and had often faced the disdain of lesser men holding higher position. After becoming ruler of all the steppe tribes, he abolished the old hereditary titles and established new ones to grant or refuse as he wished. The old aristocracy was overcome by the will and charisma of a single leader, who made merit and loyalty the prime qualifications for nobility among the Mongols.

The Mongol Aristocracy

The Mongol Empire was dominated by an aristocracy of clan leaders, appointed by Genghis Khan personally. These leaders made important decisions at the high-level assemblies known as *quriltais*. By tradition, Mongol rulers convened a *quriltai* to pass decrees, decide on war strategy, or name a successor. During the meeting, Mongol leaders spoke in order of their authority, with the most powerful speaking first. For as long as the *quriltai* lasted, all fighting and feuds were suspended, and those attending lived and ate together. By attending *quriltai*, the Mongols confirmed their support of the man who called it. By not attending, they displayed opposition or indifference.

Under Genghis Khan, the authority of the ruler and of his clan were unquestioned. The most important decisions were made by the khan personally, on the advice of his trusted counselors. Members of his immediate family were recognized as an elite, while other noble families and chiefs of the realm were subject to his rules and authority.

According to Boris Vladimirtsov, "Chingis-Khan never conceived of himself as a popular leader. He was and remained the leader of an aristocratic clan, that had unified all the Mongol aristocracy. His messages, speeches, decrees and statutes are never addressed to the people, but always to the princes, noyans [nobles], and bagaturs [elite warriors]."[19]

Genghis Khan assured the loyalty of his generals by appointing them himself and abolishing the hereditary right to noble titles. The privileged few had no independence from his authority, however. They were expected to appear at the beginning and end of the year to personally hear the khan's commands; those who failed to attend the khan's regular meetings brought themselves under suspicion. Throughout the year, the khan used a network of spies and informers to keep tabs on all of the Mongol clan leaders and nobles. If he suspected anyone of disloyalty, the suspect was summoned to his presence and tortured, if necessary, to force a confession. Genghis Khan also controlled the nobles by recruiting their sons into the keshig, his personal bodyguard. The members of this unit were, in effect, held hostage for the good behavior of their relatives.

Control of a Far-Flung Territory

The loyalty of Mongol officers and nobles served another important purpose. As the Mongol army conquered new territories, Genghis Khan chose governors from among his followers to impose Mongol rule on the conquered populations and collect tribute. With only small garrisons protecting them, the governors used the threat of Genghis Khan's return to control their subjects.

The most important weapon in the khan's arsenal was the weapon of fear, something Genghis Khan wielded as effectively as he did his well-armed horsemen.

For many conquered nations, such as Russia, Mongol rule had a long-lasting effect on society and culture. For others, the Mongols represented only a brief period of destruction and oppression. In Russia, China, and Persia, the Mongols were foreign in every way, from their habits to their clothing to the rules they lived by. No place within the empire took up the Mongol way of life, but no place they conquered ever forgot the rule of the Mongols.

The Mongol reputation for cruelty spread throughout the world, intimidating entire nations and persuading cities to surrender without a fight. Genghis Khan was happy with his very bad reputation, according to J.J. Saunders: "He deliberately set out to create a reputation for ferocious terror, in the expectation (often realized) of frightening whole nations into surrendering without resistance . . . terror was erected into a system of government to spread fear and panic and demoralize [his] enemies before a shot had been fired against them."[20]

A threatened massacre often spared Genghis Khan the need to fight and lose soldiers in a siege. Although skilled and well trained, the Mongol army was frequently outnumbered, and Genghis Khan could not spare many soldiers to occupy restive cities. With the constant campaigning, it was Mongol policy to leave a small number of Mongol governors in control before moving on. If the city then rebelled, the khan returned, leveled it to the ground, and massacred the inhabitants.

CIVILIZING THE MONGOLS

One of the most important personalities of the Mongol era was Yeh-lu Chu'tsai, a descendant of Mongol officials of the Liao dynasty, a realm established in the tenth century in northern China. Yeh-lu Chu'tsai, a scholar and shaman, fell prisoner to Genghis Khan during the siege of Zhongdu in 1215. Impressed by his knowledge and wisdom, Genghis Khan released and befriended him. On Yeh-lu Chu'tsai's advice, the khan also released native Chinese and other captives to run his growing empire.

Yeh-lu Chu'tsai convinced Genghis Khan that simply massacring defeated societies would not lead to an enduring state. He helped the Mongols set up courts of justice and taught them to use a system of measurement, paper money, and Chinese herbal medicine to prevent disease epidemics. The Mongols held him in such high esteem that after Genghis Khan's death, the khan's son Ogedei kept him in his service as the chief minister of the Mongol Empire. As much as any khan or Mongol general, Yeh-lu Chu'tsai helped transform a tribe of roving nomads and horsemen into the governors of a world empire.

This fourteenth-century illustration depicts Genghis Khan surrounded by several of his advisers.

This convinced other conquered cities to accept Mongol rule.

Seeking to make conquered territories dependent on them, the Mongols attacked economies just as efficiently as they destroyed cities. They suppressed agriculture by trampling down productive fields, burning orchards, destroying irrigation systems, and driving off peasants or herding them into their army as laborers. In all regions they conquered, they sought to create pasture for their vast horse herds, which were vital to their military campaigns. For example, when the Mongols invaded Europe in 1241, their primary objective was Hungary, where open, level grasslands, like the Mongolian steppe, would provide for their horses. Land conquered by the Mongols in what is now Iran and central Asia became a desert that has been unproductive for nearly eight centuries.

Tribute of Conquered Subjects

In conquered territories, the administration and law of the Mongols had one all important purpose: the collection of tribute, in the form of gold and goods. The Mongol defeat of the Qin dynasty in northern China brought a wealth of novel goods to the steppes: silks, jade, fine clothing, useful weapons and household goods, jewelry, precious stones, works of art, carpets, and furniture. The loot created luxury within the yurts (tents) of common soldiers as well as generals, and a strong desire for more, according to historian Jack Weatherford: "vast as the quantities were, the appetites of his own people were insatiable. As he returned from his campaigns, his caravans were laden with valuable goods, but each load created the desire for yet more. . . . Novelties became necessities, and each caravan of cargo stimulated a craving for more. The more he conquered, the more he had to conquer."[21]

Every year, each conquered territory, from China to Russia, sent a tribute of goods back to Mongolia along protected trade routes. The normal tribute was 10 percent of all the money and goods produced in a year. When the tribute arrived, precise percentages were distributed to Mongol leaders and families, according to their rank. The tribute continued so long as the fear of Genghis Khan's armies persisted. Any nation failing to send tribute to the Great Khan risked an invasion and another bloody conquest by the Mongol army.

Human captives were among the most valuable prizes for Genghis Khan. When the Mongols took cities, they often spared the lives of those with specialized skills or useful knowledge. Priests, teachers, and doctors, blacksmiths, goldsmiths, leather workers, and other artisans were brought back to the homeland to labor in the khan's service. Those who could speak foreign languages or who could read and write were also taken on as administrators and governors in the empire.

Although it exacted heavy tribute and often brought horrors and savagery, Mongol conquest also offered certain important benefits. The Mongol rulers suppressed banditry so traders and travelers could journey in safety within the Mongol khanates. The Mongols tolerated new religions in their domains and put an end to strife between different nationalities living within the same borders. Law and order imposed by the tradition of Genghis Khan's Great Yasa permitted a free flow of

The Mongols put an end to banditry in the areas they conquered, allowing travelers to journey safely from one place to another.

ideas and inventions from western Europe, through the Middle East and Persia, to central Asia and China. In the century after Genghis Khan, Europeans began their exploration of eastern Asia, by land and by sea, and new trade routes were established that allowed both sides to profit.

Communicating in the Mongol Empire

Along with the Great Yasa, which endured for centuries after Genghis Khan's death, one of his most long-lasting achievements was a system of communications and transport that survived the empire's later decline.

In the past, information in Mongolia had traveled slowly. Individual riders carried letters, goods, and orders around the steppes, always risking capture. Although protected by small corps of armed guards, merchant caravans also were the frequent target of attacks by organized groups of looters and bandits.

To keep control over his realm, Genghis Khan had to create a reliable system of sending and receiving messages. He therefore built a relay system of fast messengers, recruited from among the best riders in the army, to carry orders and information. These riders could cover 50 and sometimes 100 miles (80 to 160km) in a single day, depending on the terrain and the weather. They could spend days and nights in the saddle, carrying a little food and water and sleeping in the open if necessary.

To protect caravans and promote trade, Genghis Khan also had a series of *yams* or rest stations built across his empire. The rest stations, which lay about 20 miles (32km) apart, were run by a group of local

Rest stations called yams *were set up across the Mongol empire to protect caravans and facilitate trade. A visitor to a* yam *could obtain shelter or fresh horses.*

A *QURILTAI* SAVES EUROPE

After Kraków, Poland, fell in 1241 to the Mongols, the great horde swept south through the Carpathian Mountains and the plains of Hungary, where it defeated an army assembled by the Hungarian king. The Mongols proceeded west, to the outskirts of Vienna, preparing for an invasion of western Europe— then stopped. The fast Mongol messengers had arrived with news of the death of Ogedei, the Great Khan. According to tradition, it was time for a period of mourning and for a *quriltai* to select a successor. The Mongol generals turned their army back.

The death of a khan always required a *quriltai* to elect a successor. Even when on campaign, the generals and relatives of the khan had to call an immediate retreat in order to attend the *quriltai* in Mongolia. According to the Yasa of Genghis Khan, avoiding such a *quriltai* when summoned was a crime punishable by death, as was any attempt by a family member to claim the title of khan without the convening of the traditional assembly. The meeting called on the death of Ogedei was perhaps the most important *quriltai* ever, since it spared western Europe from the attack of a near-invincible Mongol army.

families, who maintained a stable of horses as well as an inn, where travelers could take shelter for a night or several days. In between stations, merchants could hire guards to accompany their goods and protect them (although Genghis Khan's rule greatly reduced banditry).

This system allowed merchants to conduct their business in peace, which in turn allowed artisans to produce goods and flourish. It also spread new technologies between eastern Asia and the rest of the world. Printing, firearms and gunpowder, and the use of irrigation systems and windmills were brought north from China and spread east to central Asia and Russia along Genghis

Khan's protected caravan routes. New foods such as citrus fruits and grapes arrived in China via these same routes from the orchards of Persia and the Middle East.

Far-flung conquest and trade brought the Mongols in contact with many foreign nations and other ways of life. During this turning point in Mongol history, however, the Mongol people held fast to many of their traditions. The Mongol way of life had allowed them to endure, even when surrounded by hostile tribes who were stronger and wealthier. In many respects the Mongol home survived the Mongol Empire and still suits the descendants of Genghis Khan in the twenty-first century.

CHAPTER FOUR

THE LIFE OF
THE MONGOLS

To settled peoples in China and later in central Asia, the Middle East, and Europe, the Mongols represented a kind of natural disaster to be endured and survived rather than a normal human society. The most advanced societies of the medieval age, China and Persia, looked on the Mongols as complete barbarians. The Persian chronicler Juvaini had this to say about them: "They had neither ruler nor leader. The tribes lived apart, singly or in twos . . . they lived in poverty; they wore the skins of dogs and mice, ate the flesh of these and of other dead animals."[22] Nor was a European description of the Mongols' appearance very complimentary:

[They are] hardy and strong in the breast, lean and pale-faced, rough and huge-shouldered, having flat and short noses, long and sharp chins, their upper jaws are low and declining, their teeth long and thin, their eye-brows extending from their foreheads down to their noses, their eyes inconstant [inconstant] and black, their countenances writhen and terrible, their extreme joints strong with bones and sinews, having thick and great thighs, and short legs, and yet being equal to us in

stature: for that which is wanting in their legs is supplied in the upper part of their bodies.[23]

"Civilized" nations saw the Mongols as rough barbarians, and Mongol society as unsophisticated. However, the Mongols had a complex social organization and system of family relationships. The Mongol tribes, or *irgen*, were ruled by khans and made up of several clans, known as *obok*. The clans were made up of closely related families who were exogamous: Their members always married outside the clan. The *obok* included slaves, servants, ordinary families, and members of a "first family," the *uruk*, who led the *obok* in settling disputes and in making important decisions.

Membership in the clan was open and not solely determined by blood. A Mongol could desert his clan for another and become the *nokor* (follower) of another clan leader. This was a common action during wartime, when strong leaders could win honors and treasure for their followers. It was also common for a Mongol man or woman to change clan membership through marriage. Within the clan, men drew on the tradition of *anda*, a sworn ally, who was often a friend from boyhood.

The Huns, depicted here charging into battle, were ancestors of the Mongols. Both groups were nomadic hunters and raiders.

The clan system arose from the fact that the Mongols were pastoralists, who migrated seasonally from summer plains to sheltered winter valleys and back again. The summer and winter homelands could be 100 miles (160 km) apart, and travel between them could take weeks. In such a mobile society, centralized authority was impossible. Each clan acted independently, with its own territories and

This seventeenth-century illustration depicts Mongol horsemen engaging in a hunt. To the Mongols, hunting was both a necessity and recreation.

pastures, and would fight for better ones with other clans.

When the Mongol armies settled in foreign nations, they followed this habit of the steppes. They remained nomadic hunters and herders, resisting the settled, more comfortable life of the cities. In southern Russia, conquered by the Mongols in the 1230s, the Mongols continued to migrate twice every year. In the winter, they moved south, and in the summer they moved north again. Their homes and lifestyle had been adapted to this life for centuries, and the conquest of other civilizations would not change them.

Hunting and Raiding

The Mongols remained a society of hunters even after they moved from the forests of Siberia to the grasslands of Mongolia. Hunting served several important purposes: It provided food, it trained men for war, and it was a favorite recreation. The Mongols hunted from horseback, using a sturdy bow made of yak horn and bamboo, glued with resin and bonded with silk. Iron stirrups allowed the Mongols to remain upright and steady in the saddle while pursuing their prey.

Each year, the khans would organize a "Great Hunt" for their own amusement. The hunt was started by forming a vast circle across hundreds of miles. According to the chronicler Rashid al-Din, the circle covered a distance of a month's journey. When everyone was in place, the khans sent a signal for the ring of hunters to drive the game slowly toward the center. The members of the Great Hunt then waited for their leaders to take their pick of prey. Rashid al-Din describes this moment as

practiced by Genghis Khan's son and successor Ogedei, who would

> enter the circle with his personal retinue and amuse himself for awhile killing game. When he grew tired he would ride up on to high ground in the middle of the ring, and the princes would enter in due order; then the common people and soldiers would do their killing; then some [of the animals] would be released for breeding and the rest of the game would be distributed . . . to all the various princes and emirs of the army, so that no one went without his share.[24]

When hunting was poor and food scarcer than usual, the Mongols organized raids on settlements and isolated camps. A successful raid brought in a herd of fresh animals—oxen, horses, and sheep—which provided meat and milk. In *Genghis Khan and the Making of the Modern World*, author Jack Weatherford describes this time-honored custom:

> The attackers used the same tactics in approaching human prey as animals, and at first sign of attack, the targeted victims usually fled, leaving behind most of their animals, the material goods of their homes, and whatever else the attackers might want. Since the object of the attack was to secure goods, the attackers usually looted the *gers* [tents] and rounded up the animals rather than pursuing the fleeing people.[25]

Pictured in this nineteenth-century illustration is one of Genghis Khan's many wives.

The richest prizes for any Mongol raiding party lay among the large, wealthy settlements to the south in the towns and camps. The most valuable loot belonged to the towns and camps close to the Great Wall (a series of fortified towers and walls protecting northern China) and the Silk Road (a network of trade routes linking China with central Asia and the Middle East). An ambitious raiding party took goods, animals, and young women, who were forced into marriage. A family or clan falling victim to a raiding party was honor-bound to avenge the insult and recover any stolen goods. In this way, the raids often sparked blood feuds that lasted for years. For instance, the insult offered to young Temuchin by the Merkids, who kidnapped his fiancée Borte and then left her pregnant with her first son, was avenged by Temuchin with a wholesale massacre of this people. This victory played a key role in Genghis Khan's recognition by the Mongols as their Universal Ruler.

Marriage and Family

Marriage, either by theft or by arrangement, was a crucial event in the life of any Mongol man or woman. The Mongols looked on marriage as their transition to adulthood, the gateway to full participation in society. Ties of marriage were strong among Mongol families and clans, and a wise marriage was seen as a benefit to all members of a family. For these reasons, the Mongols had important customs for choosing marriage partners and for the relations between husbands and wives.

In marriage, the Mongols sought to improve their standing in society and to gain valuable allies. Many of the crucial events in Mongol history turned on such arrangements. When he was living as the vassal of Toghrul Khan, the rising and popular Temuchin offered his eldest son Jochi in marriage to the khan's daughter. This would have made Temuchin a paramount leader himself, the successor of Toghrul Khan as leader of all the Mongols. When Toghrul Khan refused the match and then treacherously plotted Temuchin's own death, Temuchin led his followers against the elder man, defeating him and then attaining the title of Genghis Khan.

Most Mongol marriages were arranged when prospective brides were young, aged ten or even younger. For instance, Genghis Khan was betrothed to his Unggirats bride Borte at the age of nine. If a man offered marriage, he was expected to bring presents to the bride's family; if he was too poor to offer anything worthwhile, he might work in the service of his fiancée's family, sometimes for several years. On the occasion of the wedding, the bride in turn was expected to bring presents to the family of her husband. The most prized gifts were coats of marten or sable, treasures unobtainable by any but the wealthiest households. Marriage was thus a financial transaction, a source of goods and wealth for the parents. Both families exchanged gifts and vied to display their wealth, in the form of prized animals, clothing, gold coins and jewelry, and finely wrought cups, plates, and wine vessels.

The Mongols were polygamous—men took as many wives and concubines as they could support, while recognizing a favorite wife as the head of the household. This spouse enjoyed the status of "principle" or "first" wife. When they made camp, the first wife took the place of honor—by tradition, the westernmost place in the settlement—while the one of lowest rank lived on the east.

Wives and concubines were signs of high status and wealth, with the Mongol khan maintaining the largest household of them all. The khans always traveled with their wives, each of whom had her own dwelling and procession of carts. Kublai Khan, the grandson of Genghis Khan and an emperor of China, took concubinage to an extreme, with an enormous household of women whose only duty was to please their master and produce children. According to Milton Rugoff, a biographer of the Italian traveler Marco Polo:

At the palace [of Khan-Balik] lived his many concubines, who were selected at the rate of about thirty or forty every year from among the most beautiful young girls of Kungurat, a province famous for its handsome women. Each was carefully trained to serve the Great Khan, and he had so many that he would sometimes bestow one upon a noble as a reward. Far from being outraged at having their daughters chosen, parents considered it a piece of rare good fortune.[26]

While she was married, a woman held authority over the household, including the food supply and the family flocks. A Mongol woman's most important occupation was to keep herds of cattle, sheep, goats, and horses. She was also responsible for making felt, a thick mat of sheep's wool used to line outer garments and to insulate the Mongol home from the wind and cold of the steppes. Wives also cooked, sewed, reared infants and young children, and set up and took down the tents after a move between summer and winter camps.

Another vital task was to keep her husband's weapons and armor ready for a campaign. In one decree, Genghis Khan stated:

If a woman is stupid and slovenly, without understanding and without order, we see in her the bad qualities of her husband. But if she manages her household well, receives guests and messengers suitably and entertains them [with] hospitality, she enhances her husband's prestige, giving him a notable reputation in the assembly. Good men are recognised by the goodness of their wives.[27]

On the husband's death, it was the custom for his heir to take all of these wives and concubines, except for his biological mother, as his own. In this way, a household was kept together and its members were not left to fend for themselves without the protection of men. According to historian E.D. Phillips, this custom shocked outsiders, but it provided Mongol women with security: "The practice . . . was very common among the Altaic nomads [a group including the Mongols]. It gave the widows and their children security against virtual enslavement and robbery of their goods and animals."[28] Even in normal times, Mongol families faced starvation if hunting was poor or if a raid deprived them of their herds. A woman finding herself alone, without sons to assist her or family goods to offer a potential husband, could be abandoned on the steppes to forage and survive alone as best she could.

Mongol families lived a close-knit existence. Whether living in the summer or winter camps, they rarely moved far from their homes, and never left the steppes,

LIVING UNDER THE MONGOL YOKE

The taking of prisoners was often the goal of a family or clan seeking vengeance for a past wrong. Slaves were also taken in battle. Genghis Khan himself spent part of his youth as a slave in a rival clan and would have remained a slave for the rest of his life had he not escaped. A Mongol considered a slave valuable property, to be watched over at all times, defended if threatened with capture by another, or traded for more valuable items such as horses.

Mongol households restricted their prisoners' movement by placing a heavy wooden shackle known as a *cangue* across the neck. The *cangue* had small openings for the arms, which were lifted beside the head and held in place when the shackle was closed. By weighing down the shoulders and trapping the arms, the *cangue* allowed the prisoner to walk but not to use his hands, making it uncomfortable to lie down or sleep.

a fact that makes Genghis Khan's conquest of more than half of Asia even more amazing. For the Mongol family, basic needs were a bit of familiar land, a nearby river for water, and a tent that could withstand the wind and cold. They considered everything outside this world foreign and strange, while everything within had to be defended against the hostile natural elements.

The Mongol Home

Mongol homes were circular tents made of felt—matted sheep's wool—stretched over a light, portable frame of branches. To protect the felt and better insulate the home against the cold, the walls were covered with a layer of grease and a coat of lime or powdered bone. Doorways were covered with a movable flap of felt. The *ger* or yurt, as it was called, easily withstood the high winds and bitter cold of the Mongolian steppes, and it could be quickly dismantled, moved in pieces, and set up again in a different location.

Inside, the floor of the yurt was covered with felt, animal skins, or mats of woven grass or wool. Embroidered cloth with patterns of animals, birds, and trees decorated the walls. In the center of the yurt was the cooking hearth, a pit dug into the ground directly beneath a circular opening that allowed smoke to escape. A seat for the master of the house rested against the north wall, facing the entrance. The western half of the dwelling was intended for the use of family and guests, while the eastern half was the private women's quarters, used for cooking and for storage of food and utensils. Family possessions were stored in chests, while weapons, religious idols, and drying meat were hung on the walls.

There were no cities, villages, or neighborhoods among the Mongols. Instead, there were encampments, containing a few dozen yurts, each very carefully placed by its family. Related families in the clan set up their yurts within a southward-facing semicircular group. The size, decoration, and, above all, location of the yurt symbolized the social standing of Mongol families and leaders. The most respected families had the largest pens for their herds and placed their homes facing south, with a clear view of the sun.

The khans, at the top of the social ladder, lived in an encampment of their own

Durable, warm, and portable, the yurt was the primary shelter of the Mongols. The location of a yurt conveyed the social standing of the family who dwelled in it.

Inside a yurt was a central cooking hearth. Possessions were stored in chests lining the walls.

called the *ordo*. The *ordo* refers to the grand tents of the Mongol rulers, the capital of their domains and the seat of their power. Within the *ordo* (the root of the English word "horde"), the khan's home was placed in the middle, with no dwelling blocking his view to the south. The wealthiest khans furnished their homes with carpets, heavy doors, and silk hangings. They also kept treasure chests of money, jewels, and gold.

In Genghis Khan's day, the *ordo* became a movable palace, where several hundred people could meet for audiences and ceremonies. But despite this luxury, the khans of the Mongols never gave up their nomadic way of life, even after the far-flung conquests of Genghis Khan. True to his roots as a nomad, Genghis Khan moved his *ordo* with the seasons, and his sons followed this tradition.

Household Flocks and Goods

In Genghis Khan's time, valuable loot and trade goods filled the tents of rulers and generals. But the property of ordinary Mongol families remained simple: a yurt, some grazing land, and a pen for horses, sheep, and goats. The Mongol families had several carts for moving their yurt and other possessions. They built coffers of interlaced twigs, coated with felt, for their household goods. The wealthiest Mongol households might have a train of two hundred carts for everything the family owned—tents, furniture, clothing, and weapons.

The most valuable possessions of a Mongol household, however, were its animals. Horses were fed and cared for before other animals (sheep, cattle, and goats), and the daughter or son who had the responsibility for keeping them held the place of honor among all siblings. Mongolian ponies were short and sturdy, with thick, dense coats that protected them from the cold and wind of the steppes. Like camels, they needed little water, could travel for several days without a rest, and could graze on roots if necessary. From the hides of sheep, goats, horses, and oxen, the Mongols fashioned their clothing. Tallow (animal fat) was used for protecting leather and other material from the weather; horn and bone went into utensils, tools, and weapons.

In the fall, Mongol families slaughtered some of their sheep for meat for the winter months. As the temperature fell and snow covered the ground, the Mongols migrated from open summer pastures to protected mountain valleys. Ground and rivers froze solid, the days grew short, and the bitter winds from Siberia made existence difficult.

Clothing

The Mongols had been conditioned to this harsh existence by centuries of living on the steppes. They were short, stocky, and swarthy, with straight black hair. Men, who commonly wore mustaches and sparse beards, cut their hair close to the scalp with only a single lock left on the side of the head. Women combed their hair straight back and ornamented it with pendants and beads. The skin of Mongol men and women was tanned and weathered by a life spent outdoors in the sun and wind. They used animal fat, a kind of medieval sunblock, as a natural protective coating on their faces.

For clothing, men and women wore tunics made from animal skins (fancier ones were made of velvet or silk). The tunic was a long, sleeveless covering draped over the shoulders and gathered on the right side. The fur of the skin was left on and turned against the body to provide warmth. Men wore trousers tucked into leather boots. To protect against the cold, they also had a knee-length, long-sleeved coat. A belt around their waist carried a sheath for their bows, which hung at their sides, and a quiver for the arrows, which hung at the small of the back. Small furs were used to cover the shoulders and head. Dress for women was much the same, but married Mongol women always wore the *boghtaq*, a headdress made of brocade or velvet and decorated with stones, feathers, or expensive jewels. Unmarried women did not wear the *boghtaq*.

Food and Drink

Like their clothing, the diet of the Mongols was simple and well adapted to an active life in severe outdoor conditions. They grew no crops or orchards and lived on the staples of meat, milk, cheese, and millet, a grain imported from northern China, which could be boiled with milk to make a nourishing porridge. They boiled meat in large cooking pots to make a stew or simply ate it raw. When their oxen or horses died, the Mongols preserved the meat by cutting it into strips and drying it in the open air on racks. Dried oxhides were used for pouches to carry the preserved meat and other food during long journeys. Horsehides served as cooking pots when ordinary clay pots were not available.

The raw meat and water were placed inside a horsehide, which was then filled with heated rocks that boiled the flesh.

The Mongols depended on hunting and fishing to supplement their diet. Mongol hunters brought home gazelles, antelope, foxes, mountain sheep, and wild goats. With no grain, vegetables, or fruit available to them, except by trade, the Mongols subsisted largely on protein. John of Plano Carpini, a thirteenth-century European guest of the Mongols, wrote that they "have neither bread nor herbs nor vegetables nor anything else, nothing but meat. They drink mare's milk in very great quantities if they have it; they also drink the milk of ewes, cows, goats and even camels."[29] The Mongols sometimes exchanged their hides and wool for food. Despite this trade, fruit and vegetables remained very rare in the Mongol diet. When meat was not available, they gathered edible herbs and plants. On the trail, Mongol riders would sometimes resort to the blood of their horses for nourishment. Only if they were starving would Mongols consider killing a horse for food.

Modern-day Mongolian fishermen display the bounty of their catch. In Genghis Khan's empire, the Mongol diet consisted largely of animal protein.

The Mongols also consumed butter, milk, and yogurt. Churned butter was stored in sheep guts, where it never soured, while the liquid left over from the churning was allowed to go rancid, then boiled and dried into lumpy curds. Soldiers stored these curds in leather pouches as trail food. In winter, the Mongols softened the dried curds with boiled water and then drank the pungent liquor.

In the months when their sheep, goats, and horses were not producing milk, the Mongols had to preserve milk by solidifying it—allowing it to curdle. Mare's milk was fermented into koumiss. This drink was made by beating the milk in large leather bags, which separated the whey and curds, and then allowing the whey to grow bitterly sour and mildly alcoholic. Koumiss was the drink of summer; in winter the Mongols made another alcoholic drink from rice, millet, and honey. They favored wine when it was available in the countries they conquered.

Mongol Drinking

Drinking parties were common and would be arranged in all seasons for any reason. Men who could afford to keep large horse herds also considered elaborate drinking parties a sign of their wealth and prestige. William of Rubruck, another European traveler, describes the elaborate ceremony that started off a Mongol drinking party. Before the festivities began, according to Rubruck, a few drops were dedicated to a small idol that stood over the couch of the master of the household. Then,

an attendant goes out of the dwelling with a cup and liquor, and sprinkles three times to the south, each time bending the knee, and that to do reverence to the fire; then to the east, and that to do reverence to the air; then to the west to do reverence to the water; to the north they sprinkle for the dead. When the master takes the cup in hand and is about to drink, he first pours a portion on the ground. If he were to drink seated on a horse, he first before he drinks pours a little on the neck or the mane of the horse.[30]

Heavy drink was the downfall of more than one Mongol khan. Ogedei, the second Great Khan after Genghis Khan, had a weakness for binge drinking that ruined his health. Rashid al-Din relates a well-known story of how his brother Chagatai tried to set Ogedei on a different path:

Day by day he grew weaker, and though his intimates and well-wishers sought to prevent him, it was not possible, and he drank more in spite of them. Chaghatai appointed an emir . . . to watch over him and not allow him to drink more than a specified number of cups. As he could not disobey his brother's command, he used to drink from a large cup instead of a small one, so that the number remained the same. And that emir-supervisor also used to give him wine and act as a drinking companion in order to make himself one of his confidants; and so his attendance brought no benefit.[31]

THE TURTLES OF KARAKORUM

Today, the site of Karakorum, once the capital of the Mongol Empire, is an empty, grassy plain with almost no sign whatsoever that it was once a thriving capital and center of trade. The only surviving remains of Karakorum, in fact, are two large turtles, carved out of granite, which originally carried inscribed pillars on their backs.

The turtles, along with two others that have since disappeared, marked the boundaries of the Mongol capital. They were believed to protect the city from storms, floods, and human enemies. In Mongol belief, the long-lived turtle was also a symbol of eternity. In modern Mongolia, these famous turtles have become a symbol of Genghis Khan's empire and are reputed to retain their power to protect the life and health of those who come in contact with them.

This turtle sculpture is one of four that marked the boundaries of Karakorum, the capital of the Mongol Empire.

The Mongols found many occasions for drinking and celebration: weddings, births, the foaling of mares, victories in battle, a change of a season, or the meeting of leaders in a traditional *quriltai*. They considered themselves among the most fortunate of people, although in the eyes of outsiders, this Mongol life was harsh and unforgiving. Because they held to their traditional lifestyle, they were disdained by the Chinese and even by wealthier steppe societies, some of which were adopting the trappings of civilization: permanent towns, trade in goods they manufactured, and a more settled existence.

Genghis Khan and his followers resisted such "progress." They lived and died within an intricate web of alliances and kinship groups. For answers to life's most important questions and problems, they looked to spirits of the earth and sky. The most honored class among them were the shamans, who knew this world intimately and who provided a means to communicate with and know this invisible world.

MONGOL HONOR AND CHARITY

The Mongols placed honor above all other qualities. They looted with passion, but they were generous and always ready to give up their riches for the sake of honor and acclaim. Death came as easily as breathing or sleeping—in the Mongol view, gold could do little to prevent it. One Mongol ruler, Ogedei, was famous for his charity toward the poor. In Ogedei's view, the attainment of a respected name was worth more than money, and generosity was the means by which one attained such honor. In Rashid al-Din's book *The Collected Histories* the historian quotes the khan on this subject:

It is known of a certainty to all mankind that the world is faithful to none and that wisdom requires a man to keep himself alive by the perpetuation of a good name. . . . Those who strove after [riches] were devoid of their share of intellect, for no difference can be imagined between buried treasure and dust, both being of equal advantage. Since it will be impossible to return from that other world, we shall lay down our treasure in the corner of men's hearts, and whatever is ready and present or may come to hand we shall give it all.

CHAPTER FIVE

SHAMANISM AND THE ETERNAL SKY

Their long history of living as nomads, their fortunes determined by a harsh environment, gave the Mongols an accepting, fatalistic outlook. Their soldiers readily sacrificed their own lives in battle, their law codes dealt the death penalty for a variety of offenses, and their khans and generals were famous for massacring entire city populations. Life was cheap among the Mongols, even after Genghis Khan established a great empire and the Mongol court grew wealthy from tribute.

Genghis Khan imposed his will and his laws, but not his religion, on his followers and on conquered territories. This religious tolerance allowed Muslims, Christians, Buddhists, and native animists to live in Mongolia, and throughout the Mongol Empire, without conflict. Each group had its own houses of worship, where adherents could follow their rites without interference. But the foreign religions did not make much headway among Mongol families, who continued to worship the sky god Tengri and follow the teachings of traditional shamans.

Genghis Khan was seen as the chief shaman, a man blessed by the sky with good fortune and a mandate to rule his people. Although he tolerated outside religions,

he would not adopt them; although he allowed foreign holy men complete liberty, he did not follow them. There was a very practical side to this stand, as pointed out by J.J. Saunders: "Never had the continent of Asia enjoyed so complete a liberty of conscience, never had it been filled with so many ardent missionaries seeking to push their doctrines. Thus the clergy of all the competing religions tended to preach loyalty to the Mongols, a circumstance which helped to perpetuate their rule."[32]

The Mongols put their faith in the natural world, in the spirits that lived in the hills, rivers, rocks, trees, and sky. The natural world was an overpowering force that determined their good or bad fortune, the course of their lives, and even the manner of their death. This system of faith permeated the daily life of the Mongols. In the environment they knew, there was no element as powerful as the sky, which gave rise to day and night, provided rain and snow, brought storms and wind, and contained the puzzling mysteries of sun, moon, planets, and stars. The Mongols called on the sky god Tengri and the natural spirits every day for protection and placed their trust in shamans that had the power to enter this spirit world and bend it to their will.

The Mongol Spirits

The spirits of the Mongol world manifested themselves in fire and many other natural elements. They were present at the source of a river, at a prominent rock, and on a mountaintop. Any object that linked the earth and the sky became an object of reverence. Spirits could inhabit trees, for example, which sent their roots into the ground and their branches to the sky. Many of these spirits had names and personalities, which were made familiar to the Mongols through legends told by parents and other elders.

In the Mongol mythology, Nachigai was a spirit of fertility, and Otuken was the earth mother, the spirit of the earth and forests, who assured the abundance of Mongol herds and the prosperity of the clans and families. Erlik was the khan of the underworld, while the heavenly sky deity, supreme above all, was Tengri, or Mongke Tengri (the Eternal Sky). Tengri was the spirit that encompassed all existence and reigned over all life on earth. Historian Michael Hoang comments:

> The distributor of energy, he is to be seen in cataclysmic phenomena; in messages carried by animals that manifest themselves in supernatural forms, and in "signs of destiny." Tenggeri can spurn the pleadings of one who intercedes with him; he can bring death. He even has the power to channel his energy and convert it to secondary forces. He is both the guardian of the universal order and the primary cause of a "Great All."[33]

To gain the favor of Tengri, Mongol shamans and leaders would retreat to a high hill or mountaintop, where they would spend several days in meditation. Before a military campaign, a hunt, and the vital season of milking mares, the khans and shamans made an offering of the fermented milk of white mares to Tengri.

Along with the spirits of the earth and sky, the Mongols believed in a soul that existed within yet apart from the physical body. Illness or bad luck resulted from the loss of balance between body and soul. Violent death, in turn, could give rise to the haunting of survivors by the spirits of the dead. For help with unwanted spirits and other ill fortune, the Mongols turned to the most respected members of their society, the shamans.

The Work of Shamans

The Mongol shamans were gifted with supernatural sight. These shamans were always men, and Mongol herdsmen, soldiers, artisans, nobles, and khans all respected the shamans and believed in their abilities. The khans excused the shamans from fighting in the army and gave them a privileged position at the courts. By the decrees of the Great Yasa, Genghis Khan made all priests and holy men exempt from taxation and any form of public service.

A shaman understood and communicated with the unseen spirit world. He also possessed a deep knowledge of Mongol history that was passed down from one shaman to the next. According to historian Peter Brent:

> The *shaman* was the intermediary between man and the gods, his vocation either hereditary, or sudden

Mongol shamans like the one pictured in this illustration were believed to communicate with the spirit world.

and peculiar to him. Ecstatic dream trained him, and his elders passed on to him their technical knowledge—the names of the spirits and what they did, the mythology and the genealogical descent of the clan and its leaders, the special language that kept shamanistic knowledge secret from the world.[34]

The shamans dealt with spirits of all kinds and, like the khans, served as intermediaries between earth and heaven. The Mongol word for "shaman" is *bo*, adapted from the Turkish word *bogu*, which means "wizard" or "magician." The shaman was a medium between the otherworldly spirits of the sky and the mountains and the ordinary, visible world. He could tell the future, heal the sick, cause rain to fall, assist the khans in battle, and bring good fortune to anyone undertaking an important or difficult task.

Most shamans took up the calling of their fathers. Certain Mongol families provided the clans with shamans, one generation after the next, with experienced fathers and grandfathers training their sons. The apprentice learned spells and incantations, how to use magic to heal, the art of fortune-telling, and the location of powerful places—mountaintops, springs, and deserts where the spirits could be seen and felt directly.

A strange, mystical experience always marked the entry of an apprentice shaman into the ranks. Such an event was described by a contemporary Mongol shaman to the author Stanley Stewart, who ventured into modern Mongolia to explore the homeland of Genghis Khan's empire:

Though he always knew he would be a shaman, the powers did not manifest themselves until he was thirty-seven. . . . He became dizzy, and had fainting spells, shortness of breath, and convulsions as the spirits began to whisper their entreaties. He was in bed for a fortnight, troubled by bizarre dreams and a raging fever. When he came round he knew the spirits had captured him, and his life as a shaman had begun.[35]

One of the most useful of the shaman's abilities was telling the future. Shamans were enlisted before every great undertaking, such as a migration to new pastures or a military campaign. They interpreted the signs given by the spirits and in this way prepared listeners to deal with forthcoming events. The shamans' abilities as fortune-tellers made them most useful to the khans of the Mongols, who depended on these signs to guide them in decisions that would affect the entire nation.

The Shamans of the Court
The Mongol khans kept several of the most powerful shamans in their court. These shamans acted as guides and soothsayers, attended the khans, led them while on the move, and helped them find the best place for their dwellings. The shamans were also responsible for taking care of religious images, which were set up in places of honor in the khan's *ordo*, or palace tent.

The chief of the shamans was known as the *beki*. The *beki* held a place of honor in a Mongol encampment; Genghis Khan himself allowed his chief shaman to camp directly in front of his own royal tent.

THE GREAT DEBATE

In Mongolia, Muslims, Christians, and Buddhists all practiced their faith and asked for the favor of the khans. To settle religious differences, the khans often summoned the leaders of the different faiths to debate the virtues and weaknesses of their beliefs. One of these debates, held in 1254 before the Great Khan Mongke, was described by William of Rubruck in his book *Journey of William Rubruck*:

> We were assembled then on Pentecost eve at our oratory, and Mangu [Mongke] Chan sent three secretaries who were to be umpires, one a Christian, one a Saracen, and one a Tuin [Buddhist]; and it was published aloud: This is the order of Mangu, and let no one dare say that the commandment of God differs from it. And he orders that no one shall dare wrangle or insult any other, or make any noise by which this business shall be interfered with, on penalty of his head. Then all were silent. And there was a great concourse of people there; for each side had called thither the most learned of its people, and many others had also assembled.

William records that the debate ended with a draw. "They all listened without making any contradiction, but no one said: 'I believe; I want to become a Christian.' . . . When this was over, the Nestorians [Christians] as well as the Saracens sang with a loud voice; while the Tuins kept silence, and after that they all drank deeply."

The *beki* had the privilege of wearing white clothing and of receiving the offerings of clan leaders and khans. He exercised political power as well as religious authority. He could abuse this power by accusing a rival of practicing witchcraft and turning him over to the khan for trial and punishment.

The Mongol khans always enlisted the shamans in preparations for a battle. Invoking the sky god, the protector of the Mongols, shamans held ceremonies and made offerings to the spirits. By their incantations, they turned the weather favorably to their own side and called down bad fortune on opposing commanders. They also used scapulimacy (predicting the future by studying the shoulder blades of sheep) to predict the outcome of the coming battle. This was a fortune-telling method honed through the centuries by the Mongol shamans. By burning the shoulder blades of sheep and then examining the pattern of cracks in the bone

This illustration shows Genghis Khan consulting a shaman to determine the most auspicious day for engaging an enemy in battle.

that resulted, the shamans decided on the best days for undertaking a seasonal migration, fighting a battle, or laying siege to an enemy city.

These rites of fortune-telling were conducted within temples. The temples were surrounded by sanctified grounds; the temple gate always lay on the southern side, with a long pole set up to mark the spot. The temples were large tents, laid out with a small alcove on the north side, where a small altar held idols, lamps and offerings. On the walls were images of natural spirits, often in the form of animals or demons, and scripts in the Uighur lettering used by the Mongols to write their language. The shamans enforced silence in the temples, saying nothing and allowing no one to speak.

Religion in Daily Life

The *beki*, the ordinary shamans, and even the khan created a link between the Mongols and the unseen spirits. These men told and sang legends as a way of instructing the Mongol people—most of whom could not read or write—about the spirit world. But the basic beliefs of the Mongols were passed on within families, which, as in many Asian societies, worshipped their ancestors.

All Mongol families had several small *ongghon* (images) set up in their household.

THE ASTROLOGERS OF KARAKORUM

Among the Mongols of Genghis Khan's time, a busy trade was carried on by astrologers. Many of them were Arabic-speaking Muslims who had been invited by the khan and by his nobles to Karakorum. These astrologers served in the khan's court and in other wealthy households, casting horoscopes for newborns and advising on aspects of the stars and planets that affected their patrons' fortunes in battle, the proper alignment of their homes, or the best day and time to set out on a journey. For those who could read, almanacs were compiled by the astrologers. In these books they tracked the movement of planets, the moon, and the constellations and made their predictions about weather, natural disasters, and important human events such as wars, royal successions, and civil disturbances. The most accurate of these books gained their authors wide renown.

The astrologers of Mongolia enjoyed a far-ranging reputation. Although the Chinese had little respect for Mongol civilization, they greatly admired the abilities of Genghis Khan's astrologers. After the khan's death, many astrologers journeyed south to China, where they would have a permanent influence on Chinese methods of geomancy and divination.

These figures symbolized their ancestors. The Mongols believed that the *ongghon*, if properly cared for, would provide protection to the family. The *ongghon* could be made of wood, silk, felt, or stone. Some were placed near the seats of the husband and principal wife, and others placed near the door of the yurt. When the family was on the move, the *ongghon* were set up in special carts that were carefully maintained and guarded.

In his memoir of the time he spent among the Mongols, William of Rubruck described the *ongghon* as well as the Mongol shamans who guarded them:

> The . . . Tartars who are of this sect, though they believe in one God, make nevertheless images of their dead in felt, and dress them in the richest stuffs, and put them in one or two carts, and no one dare touch these carts, which are under the care of their soothsayers, who are their priests. . . . These soothsayers are always before the ordu of Mangu [a Great Khan and a descendant of Genghis Khan] and of other rich people, for the poor have none, but only those of the family of Chingis [Genghis Khan]. And when they are on the march, these [soothsayers] precede them as the pillar of a cloud did the children of Israel, and they decide where to pitch the camp, and when they have set down their dwellings, all the ordu follows them.[36]

Along with the *ongghon* images, the Mongols provided themselves with further protection in the form of a central fire, which was kept burning at all times. Besides providing heat for the yurt and for cooking, the fire symbolized the health and endurance of the entire household. The Mongols believed that allowing the fire to go out brought bad fortune. One could not walk over the fire, spill anything into it, or allow ordinary knives, weapons, or tools to touch it. The fire purified objects that came in contact with it, and an important funeral custom was to have mourners pass between two fires to cleanse them of earthly pollutions. When moving to a new home, the Mongols started the new fire with an ember of the old one. Brides and grooms brought fire from their old household to the new one, to symbolize the joining of two families.

There were many fire rituals carried out on a regular basis—daily, monthly, seasonally, and yearly—by every Mongol family. As a living organism, fires had to be fed; one traditional mixture was fried millet mixed with sugar and butter. At the end of the lunar year, all families held a ceremony around their fires to prepare for the first month of the new year.

Religious ceremony accompanied birth, marriage, the seasonal migration, and the acclamation of new clan leaders and khans. Important events such as these were sanctified and blessed with the incantations of shamans, who ensured the favor of spirits and of the god of the sky. The most solemn and elaborate such occasion was the ceremony following death, when the spirit escaped the body and took up a new home in the unseen world.

Funerals

For the Mongols, death was a very familiar event. A Mongol family slaughtered herd

THE EIGHT WHITE YURTS

Just as Mongol families worshipped their ancestors, the Mongol nation venerated Genghis Khan after his death in 1227. The cult of Genghis Khan centered on eight of his worldly possessions: the three yurts of his wives, the remains of his white horse, his arrows and quivers, the reins and saddle of his horse, his milk pail, and a collection of his writings. These objects were kept in small, square yurts and transported on carts from place to place in Mongolia through the centuries. They were carefully guarded by a group of five hundred families, known as the Dark-had, whose sole task was to keep the cult objects and prevent any interference with them by outsiders. Four times a year, the Mongols would make a ceremonial sacrifice at the white yurts.

The cult objects of Genghis Khan, including the coffin supposedly containing his remains, lasted through centuries of war, civil strife, and invasion by outsiders. In the 1950s, they were placed in a mausoleum erected by the People's Republic of China. During China's Cultural Revolution, when the Chinese government sought to erase artifacts of the past, members of China's Red Guards broke into the mausoleum and destroyed the relics, which have since been replaced by copies.

Artifacts belonging to Genghis Khan were kept in this Chinese mausoleum until they were destroyed during China's Cultural Revolution.

animals regularly; the hunting of animals was necessary for survival, fatal sickness and accidents were common, especially among children, and violence often resulted in death. The Mongols accepted these circumstances and rarely feared death. Their funerals were common, almost everyday rituals, surrounded by many familiar and longstanding traditions.

Chieftains were buried with their possessions, their favorite animals, and their weapons. It was the practice among some tribes to kill the wives and servants of important deceased leaders and bury them in the same grave to accompany the chiefs in the next world. Among the Mongols of the Golden Horde, in what is now Ukraine and

This stone grave marker indicates the burial site of a Mongol king in South Korea.

A REVERENCE FOR ALL FAITHS

Religion was a practical matter to the Mongol rulers, even after the death of Genghis Khan, who decreed religious tolerance throughout his realm. On the feast days of the Christians—Easter and Christmas—Kublai Khan would have the Gospels brought into his presence. Reverence was paid to the Christian holy books by burning incense over them, after which the khan would kiss the books and have his nobles and princes do the same. He paid the same homage to the holy books of the Muslims and Jews. In *The Travels*, the Italian merchant Marco Polo quotes the khan as saying:

Genghis Khan is shown in the pulpit of a mosque in this fourteenth-century illustration.

There are four prophets who are worshipped and to whom all the world does reverence. The Christians say that their God was Jesus Christ, the Saracens Mahomet, the Jews Moses, and the idolators Sakyamuni Burkhan, who was the first to be represented as God in the form of an idol. And I do honour and reverence to all four, so that I may be sure of doing it to him who is greatest in heaven and truest; and to him I pray for aid.

southern Russia, the funerary habits of the western steppes were adopted. A horse was driven over and over the site of the tomb until it died of exhaustion. The horse was then gutted and its skin was impaled on a long pole above the grave. The horse skin may have been intended to frighten away

evil spirits from the site or it may have been an offering to Tengri.

By tradition, however, death and Mongol funerals were not meant to be long remembered. A funeral was a way to conceal the fact of death; one of the gravest insults one could offer to the dead was to leave them exposed to decay in the open. The Mongols quickly buried their dead and, for those they most respected, took great care to conceal the tomb. They carefully restored any disturbed earth and grass so that the spot could not be found again. No grave markers, stones, or inscriptions marked the graves. Instead, the Mongols allowed earth and nature to do their work and hide the graves from curious eyes. Those who took part in the funeral of a man of importance might be killed themselves to prevent others from finding the grave site. One description of a Mongol funeral was given by the Persian historian Juvaini:

> Among that people it is the usage, when one of them dies, to prepare a place under ground about the size of a chamber or hall, in largeness proportionate to the rank and degree. . . . They furnish it with a throne and covering for the ground, and they place there vessels and numerous effects, together with his arms and weapons, and whatever may have been his own private property, and some of his wives and slaves, male or female, and the person he loved most above all others. . . . In the night-time the place is covered up, and horses are driven over it, in such a manner that not a trace of it remains.[37]

Encounters with New Faiths

The Mongol funeral traditions endured throughout Genghis Khan's empire, even though many new faiths and religious customs arrived on the steppes. Having conquered much of the known world, the khan was now learning the doctrines of European Christians, of the Muslims of central Asia and the Middle East, and of Chinese Buddhists and Taoists. In these new faiths he sought answers to profound questions and eventually came to the conclusion that, in the old Chinese adage, "many roads lead to heaven."

The Mongol capital of Karakorum contained temples of several other faiths. Christian churches, Islamic mosques, and Buddhist temples were often crowded with worshippers. At a time when religion was giving rise to violent civil strife in Europe, the Middle East, and elsewhere in Asia, the Mongol Empire offered religious toleration. Genghis Khan set the standard for this policy by his own actions, according to an account of his life on The Mongols Web site: "[He] consulted with . . . Daoist holy men, who he hoped could provide him with an elixir that would make him immortal. . . . He was visited by Muslim mullahs, Buddhist and Daoist monks, and Christian missionaries. The followers of these faiths, as well as smaller religious communities, such as the Jews and Zoroastrians, worshipped without fear of persecution throughout his empire."[38]

The Mongols believed that something of value could be taken from each of these other faiths. The toleration of the Mongols for Christianity and other religions also arose from their belief that mere mortals, no matter how fervent, could never be certain of the true nature of things. The Mongols found something new in the promise of an afterlife, as in Islam and Christianity, and in the reincarnation of Buddhism—concepts that were foreign to their own shamanism.

THE TRANCES OF GENGHIS KHAN

For Genghis Khan, the Mongol system of belief could never be questioned. At crucial moments in his life, he retreated to sacred hilltops, deprived himself of food and comfort, meditated on his future, and fell into a trance in the search for guidance from the natural world. In the belief of the Mongols, such a trance allowed an important person to temporarily become a shaman himself, taking on the abilities of the soothsayers. Genghis Khan's encounters with the spirit world were described by the Persian historian Juvaini in John Andrew Boyle's *The Mongol World Empire 1206–1370*:

> Every now and again he used to fall into a trance, and in that state of insensibility all sorts of things used to proceed from his tongue, and that state of trance used to be similar to that which had happened to him at the outset of his rise, and the devils who had power over him foretold his victories. . . . Whenever this inspiration came over him, every circumstance—victories, undertakings, the appearance of enemies, the defeat and reduction of countries—anything which he might desire, would all be uttered by his tongue. A person used to take the whole thing down in writing and enclose it in a bag and place a seal upon it, and when Chingiz Khan came to his senses again, they used to read his utterances over to him one by one; and according to these he would act, and more or less, indeed, the whole used to come true.

To the Mongols, the God of Christianity and Islam was simply another guise of Tengri, the Eternal Sky. This god had given the earth to the Mongols to rule, through the person of Genghis Khan, and heard the prayers of all faiths.

The Mongol conquests and the policy of religious tolerance gave rise to a great religious ferment in many regions of Asia. Western China became primarily Muslim, while a Mongol dynasty survived in northern India and adopted Islam. In China, Tibetan Buddhism arose to challenge Taoism, which was suppressed under the rule of Kublai Khan, Genghis Khan's grandson and the founder of the Yuan dynasty. In Mongolia, Genghis Khan's people still paid reverence to the shamans and held on to their beliefs and rituals. They continued to believe that Genghis Khan possessed supernatural gifts to rival the most powerful of the Mongol shamans.

In Genghis Khan's later years, as his body weakened and he suffered illness, the Universal Ruler tried to prepare the Mongols for his passing. He chose a successor from among his unruly and contentious sons and saw to it that the Great Yasa was implemented in all territories under Mongol rule.

His legacy was the largest empire in history, a realm that his people, over a short period of time, found themselves incapable of holding together. The Mongol Empire, as it turned out, was very much the work of a single man, who had successfully turned the Mongols into conquerors but could not hand down the secrets of his tremendous energy, wisdom, and charisma.

CHAPTER SIX

THE DECLINE OF THE MONGOL EMPIRE

As he neared death, Genghis Khan realized that no single man could control the huge Mongol Empire and that his sons and his people lacked important qualities needed to keep his empire intact. In his book *Genghis Khan: The Rise, Authority, and Decline of Mongol Power*, historian Peter Brent speculates on the Universal Ruler's thoughts as follows: "When expansion halted and other men's riches no longer flowed into Mongol hands, what would be the purpose of the chieftain's life? Genghis Khan knew the answer to that question—there would be no purpose. The Mongols would grow fat, they would become lazy, they would forget their heritage of movement, toughness, simplicity."[39]

Genghis Khan also faced a more immediate problem in determining who would succeed him. There was no law among the Mongols that specified who would inherit his title of Great Khan. His sons were bitterly contesting control of his empire, and each had gathered a faction to support his claim. The rivalry between his second son, Chagatai, and Jochi, the eldest son (who was illegitimate), threatened all-out civil war if the family could not come to an agreement.

To avoid a war over the succession, Genghis Khan decided to distribute his conquests evenly among his heirs. Each would have a domain independent of the others, and above them all would sit the next Great Khan, who would make the decisions about going to war and have the final say in matters affecting the entire Mongol Empire. Realizing that none of his sons had his own energy and charisma, he favored Ogedei as Great Khan for this son's ability to persuade and befriend. According to E.D. Phillips, "Chingis nominated Ogodei because of his shrewd understanding of men and because of his amiable character, which would win willing obedience from others who would carry on the system."[40]

Normally, the Mongols did not discuss death, inheritance, and succession in public—these subjects were taboo according to their religious beliefs. But Genghis Khan went against this tradition by convening a *quriltai* shortly before his death. At this assembly, Genghis Khan proclaimed Ogedei as the new Great Khan of the Mongols and divided the empire among his other descendants. Batu, the son of his eldest son, Jochi, received the Middle East, Persia, and the

This fourteenth-century illustration depicts Genghis Khan and his sons, who argued bitterly over who would succeed him.

western steppes of Ukraine and southern Russia (a region Batu would still have to conquer); Chagatai received central Asia, from the Aral Sea to Mongolia, a realm known as the Chagatai Khanate; and Tolui became overlord of Mongolia.

The Mongols would always hold the memory of Genghis Khan in deep reverence. But they also found themselves, as a nation, unprepared to expand or control the huge realm he had conquered. They could not fulfill his dream of a universal Mongolian domain, where all would pay tribute to his heirs. Within a few generations after his death, the Mongol Empire declined and broke apart, while the Mongols retreated to their ancient homeland on the steppes.

The Death of Genghis Khan

On August 18, 1227, while on campaign in China, Genghis Khan died. The cause of his death is unknown—most historians believe he died of a lingering illness, while others believe he died of injuries after falling off his horse. His legacy was the conquest, in less than twenty years, of the largest realm in history. The Mongols honored him with a majestic procession from the distant Hsia-Hsia kingdom of western China, where he died, to his homeland in the Mongolian steppes. The Mongols wanted no witnesses to this solemn procession—on the way home they slew every foreigner they encountered.

After arriving in Mongolia, the body was brought to the slopes of Burkhan Khaldun. This mountain, the scene of many important events of his youth, had been made into a forbidden zone by Genghis Khan (it remained forbidden to the outside world until the twentieth century). The mourners laid his body in a wagon and then buried it on the mountain slopes under a solitary tree. Pavilions were raised for mourners and for shrines erected in Genghis Khan's memory. According to some legends, the members of the funeral party were then put to death, so that the location of the tomb would always remain a secret. The actual burial site of Genghis Khan remains unknown in the twenty-first century and has become one of the great puzzles of archaeology. The government of Mongolia, sensitive to cultural and religious taboos, has refused permission to outsiders seeking to find the tomb. According to a legend in Mongolia, the tomb is well protected by a variety of natural and supernatural guardians and will never be found.

The death of Genghis Khan began an official two-year period of mourning, as prescribed by his chief minister, Yeh-lu Chu'tsai. At the end of this time, the family of Genghis Khan assembled for a forty-day carnival of hunting, feasting, and drinking. An election then took place, with the courtiers spending each of the days in different colored clothing (this tradition had begun after the looting of the Qin dynasty, which brought a wealth of fine silks and clothing—much of it in colors the Mongols had never seen before—north to the steppes). According to Genghis Khan's declared wish, the assembly selected Ogedei as the next Great Khan.

Ogedei and the other descendants honored the memory of Genghis Khan and held to the Great Yasa, the code of law meant to make the vast conquest permanent. But none of these descendants could match the Universal Ruler's strength of mind and will. Few were effective leaders; many were greedy or incompetent or both.

The Mongols were excellent soldiers, but their tradition of conquest and looting did not prepare them as administrators. Eventually the Mongol governors found themselves challenged, and finally overthrown, by the same settled and "corrupt" (in their eyes) civilizations that had been utterly defeated and subdued by Genghis Khan and his generals.

The Palace of Ogedei

Ogedei much enjoyed the comfort and luxury feared by Genghis Khan. On his accession in 1230, he established something new for the Mongols—a permanent city. He placed the new capital of Karakorum at a site on the Orkhon River, to the west of Genghis Khan's old headquarters at Avarga. Ogedei summoned wise men from all corners of the empire, including Confucian scholars from China, engineers from Persia, and Buddhist teachers and monks. He set up an administration and legal system intended to keep the far-flung realm peaceful and prosperous.

Ogedei was no Universal Ruler or world conqueror, however. He was satisfied to enjoy the rich inheritance received from his father and live a life of ease. To create a lasting symbol of the empire's wealth and power, he ordered artisans from north China to raise a new palace, known as Wan'an-gong, or "Palace of Ten-Thousandfold Peace," which would be the largest structure in Mongolia. In the middle of the palace, facing south in the traditional Mongol style, was the elaborate pavilion of the Great Khan. Around the palace were the houses of Ogedei's relatives, including his brothers and sons, which were joined to the main palace by gardens and paths.

Beginning in the late 1940s, excavations by Russian archaeologists at Karakorum revealed that Ogedei's palace was built over a platform of earth measuring about 180 by 148 feet (55 by 45m). The building was supported by six rows of pillars set into granite bases. According to ancient accounts, it was floored and roofed with glazed tiles, while statues of dragons and other animals decorated its exterior walls, pillars, and roof. Inside, the walls were covered by fresco paintings, created by applying a mixture of wet plaster and paint directly to the wall surface.

William of Rubruck described the palace at Karakorum as a city within the city. The structure reminded him of a church, with a long central hall flanked by two long aisles. In the middle of the building was a fountain, built by a European silversmith named William the Parisian to supply the khan and the members of his court with their favorite drinks:

At its roots are four lions of silver, each with a conduit through it, and all belching forth white milk of mares. And four conduits are led inside the tree to its tops, which are bent downward, and on each of these is also a gilded serpent, whose tail twines round the tree. And from one of these pipes flows wine, from another *cara cosmos*, or clarified mare's milk, from another *bal*, a drink made with honey, and from another rice mead, which is called *terracina*; and for each liquor there is a special silver bowl at the foot of the tree to receive it.[41]

This Buddhist monastery was built in the late sixteenth century on the site of Karakorum, the Mongolian capital established by Ogedei.

Although many Mongols settled into city life in Karakorum, many more preferred to keep to their traditional nomadic lifestyle, as depicted in this illustration.

Like all the Mongol rulers, Ogedei was a great lover of drink and merriment, according to the Persian chronicler Rashid al-Din:

And when he was on his way to Qara-Qorum, there was a tall pavilion which he had built 2 parasangs (about 6 miles) [10 km] from the town named Tuzghu-Baliq; here he would . . . make merry for one day. Then on the next day the people would don garments of one color,

and he would proceed from thence to Qarshi [the palace at Karakorum], where tender youths would stand before him and for the space of a month he would devote to pleasure. He would open the doors of the treasuries and cause noble and base to share his general bounty; and every night he would pit archers, crossbowmen, and wrestlers against one another and would show favor and make presents to the winners.[42]

Daily Life in the New Capital

The majority of Mongols did not settle down to a comfortable life in Karakorum, however. Instead, the city served largely as an administrative and trade center, where tribute was collected and distributed, valuables were bought and warehoused, and artisans set up workshops to produce manufactured goods. The Saracen (Muslim) quarter held the public markets, while the Chinese quarter was the neighborhood of artisans. Archaeologists in Karakorum have unearthed red bricks still bearing the marks of the factories where they were made, as well as pipes used for the underground heating of the palace and wealthy homes. Digging at the site of homes and workshops unearthed tools, pottery fragments, wheel hubs, coins, ornaments, utensils, and weapons made or used in the thirteenth century.

Scientists have also traced a canal from the Orkhon River leading into the city. Water from the canal powered mills and waterwheels used in blacksmith shops. One excavated house, known as the Crossroads House, contained a steel forge, which was powered by a waterwheel driven by the canal. This house, excavated by archaeologists in the twentieth century, served as a factory for the residents of the city.

Although they were able to raise a functioning city, the Mongols were unable to completely surrender their identity as nomadic steppe-dwellers. Outside the walls, the imperial family kept their vast herds of horses, cattle, and sheep. Ordinary Mongol families set up their yurts as they always had, on the open steppes, and grazed their sheep and horses. They avoided settled farming and migrated with the seasons—as did Ogedei and his royal court, which wandered to different palaces and encampments throughout the year.

The Mongols did lose their taste for military conquest, however. Their armies were increasingly made up of mercenaries and conscripts, who felt no loyalty to their officers or to the cause of the Mongol Empire. Nor could the Mongols turn the inhabitants of settled, agrarian societies into nomads and herders—they could never permanently impose Mongolian ways and traditions in a place such as China, which had been one of the world's wealthiest societies well before the arrival of Genghis Khan.

The result was stagnation and a slow decline, as foreign civilizations gradually lost their fear of the Mongol armies and reclaimed their cities. Tribute to the Mongol treasury at Karakorum lessened when the most distant outposts of the empire defied the Great Khan's authority over them. In many places, popular revolts forced Mongol administrators and garrisons to retreat and return control to native governors.

The First Defeat of the Mongol Army

The descendants who followed Ogedei found themselves hard-pressed to hold the far-flung empire together and rule their millions of subjects with a few thousand Mongol officials and an army of cavalry. According to historian David Morgan,

> The Mongol khanates in the lands of ancient sedentary civilizations, Persia and China, were the first to collapse. It was easier for the Mongols to retain control where, as in the Golden Horde [of Russia] and the Chaghatai Khanate [of central Asia],

Kublai Khan, the grandson of Genghis Khan, established China's Yuan dynasty in 1279.

they were also able to maintain their ancestral nomadic way of life and hence their military supremacy over the subject populations.[43]

In the Middle East, Hulegu, a grandson of Genghis Khan, established the Ilkhanate in 1255. This realm was often at war with the domain of another grandson, Batu Khan, which lay north of the Caucasus Mountains. These realms undertook no further conquest, instead using their armies to fight against each other and to put down uprisings within their borders.

In 1260, a Mongol army suffered defeat at the hands of an Egyptian army at Ayn Jalut, near Nazareth in what is now Israel. This defeat pushed the Mongols back to the Euphrates River. In the years to come, Mongol armies were repulsed from northern India and resisted in the Caucasus region. More important for the survival of Mongol civilization, the Ilkhans of Persia converted to Islam and gradually lost their identity as Mongols.

The limits of Mongolian conquest had been reached, and the consequences were ultimately fatal. As one historian remarks, "No stability seemed possible without the stimulus of aggressive war; once that ceased, the loss of vitality and purpose became all too apparent, and decline was swift."[44]

Collapse of the Yuan Dynasty

The Mongols ruled China as the Yuan dynasty, established by Genghis Khan's grandson Kublai Khan, in 1279. This ruler united northern and southern China and established important reforms. The new dynasty seized the properties of landowners and doled them out to landless farmers. A public welfare system supported those unable to work or provide for themselves. The trade routes protected by the Mongols allowed trade between China and the rest of the world and brought prosperity, according to historian Peter Brent:

The Mongol connection stretched westward into Europe; the consequently augmented trade enriched the merchants. . . . In order to make sure that wealth should not be too

unevenly distributed, the empire's administration not only supervised the apportionment of land, it made sure that commodity prices had a ceiling that no one was allowed to exceed. Rich trade, enough land and maximum prices, the sick, the old and the poor provided for—after forty years of war, the people must have felt that their new ruler had brought them paradise.[45]

But the Yuan emperors of the fourteenth century, after the time of Kublai Khan, imposed heavy taxes and restrictions on China's merchants and farmers. Earthquakes and floods, as well as the seizure of productive land for pasture, led to widespread famine, especially in northern China. The conscription of laborers to build temples and palaces and to serve in the army and navy further hurt the peasantry. There were no laws preventing the landowners from mistreating the peasants, whose resentment at their slavelike conditions grew increasingly bitter.

At the same time, the Mongol army weakened. With their skills as archers and horsemen no longer necessary, many Mongol soldiers had become slave owners and sedentary farmers—a profession completely alien to Mongol tradition. Mongol farming estates often failed, since the Mongols had no experience of breaking the soil or the hard labor of planting, irrigating, and harvesting. Many Mongols in northern China gave up farming to wander the countryside as vagrants or bandits.

In the homeland of Mongolia, the nomads and hunters still felt a strong contempt for a civilization they saw as soft and useless.

THE ORDERLY CAPITAL OF YUAN CHINA

The Yuan emperors of China carried on many traditions learned from the very strict law of their honored ancestor, Genghis Khan. In the capital of Khan Balik, order and cleanliness prevailed. Thieves, curfew-breakers, trespassers, and other miscreants were either thrown into prison or taken outside the walls and executed. All bloodshed, in particular the killing of animals, was strictly forbidden within the city walls, as were burials. Every three years, the khan declared a general amnesty, but former prisoners would always be recognized by the brands burned into their faces. In *The Travels*, a journal of Marco Polo's wanderings through Asia, the Italian writer describes the official punishment given to children: "If it should happen that a child does anything to displease his parents or fails to remember them in their need, there is a department of state whose sole function it is to impose severe penalties on those who are found guilty of such ingratitude."

Strict laws helped ensure that the people of Khan Balik kept their city clean and orderly.

A wide rift opened between native Mongolians and the new generation of Mongol settlers in China. In Peter Brent's words,

> This hostility [of the Chinese] was matched by that of a sizeable faction among the Mongols themselves who, like Genghis Khan before them, regarded the silks and literature and fine brushwork of this civilization with a puritanical horror. Real men lived in tents, rode hard and fought harder, killed their enemies and fathered their children; their recreation was hunting and *koumiss* and uncomplicated song. Everything on the Chinese side of the Great Wall was dangerous, corrupting, sapping of the nomad will.[46]

The decline of authority of the Yuan emperors inspired peasant uprisings, which grew gradually stronger and more violent through the middle of the fourteenth century. In the 1360s, the peasant leader Chu Yuan-chang campaigned against Beijing, the Yuan capital. In 1368, at the approach of Chu Yuan-chang's armies, the last Yuan emperor, Toghan Temur, simply fled the city for Karakorum, the old capital city of the Mongolian steppes.

Chu Yuan-chang declared the founding of the Ming ("brilliant") dynasty, ending Mongol rule in China. Twenty years later, a Ming army pursuing the Mongols into their homeland completely destroyed the city of Karakorum, leaving no trace of the old capital above ground. The Mongols retreated to their homeland north of China, although the Ming emperors accepted Mongolian warriors into their army. The condition of these survivors is described by historian E.D. Phillips:

> The first Ming emperors willingly accepted into their own armies Mongols who had surrendered or been captured. They even kept them as far as possible in the same units and under the same commanders, if these were not too high in rank or lineage. These Mongols, with their families, appear to have formed separate military communities wherever they were stationed. On the northern border special commanderies of partly immigrant Mongol soldiers were settled.[47]

Outside the Mongol homelands, the title of Great Khan, first assumed by Genghis Khan in 1206, now carried no authority whatsoever. The Mongol realm split into independent principalities, each of which went its own way with no direction from Mongolia, China, or any other Mongol stronghold in the east. In Mongolia, Genghis Khan's dream of world conquest became an honored, distant memory.

The Empire Divides and Falls

Many lands of central and western Asia had been ravaged by the conquests of Genghis Khan in the early thirteenth century. Cities and fields still lay in ruins, unproductive and empty of people. Communications faltered and many petty states arose, under the control of Turkish and Arab rulers who paid no allegiance to Mongol khans anywhere. In regions where the people were still ruled by Mongols, resistance strengthened.

This illustration depicts the court of the khan Ghazan, who ruled parts of the Mongol Empire in the Middle East.

In the Middle East, the administration of the Ilkhanate grew weak and corrupt. The Mongols imposed harsh taxes to rebuild the towns and cities destroyed by their conquest and forced many poor farmers and town-dwellers into slave labor gangs. Ghazan, the khan of the Ilkhanate for ten years, ended the tradition of religious tolerance by imposing Islam and sharia, traditional law based on the Koran, the holy book of the Muslims. He thus made enemies of the Jews, Christians, and Buddhists who made up a large segment of the population. Ghazan also angered his allies among the Mongols by banning Genghis Khan's Great Yasa and traditional Mongol shamanism within his realm.

The ancient cultures of Persia and Iraq would not accept Mongol language and culture, which would always seem alien and strange to them. In the words of historian J.J. Saunders,

Barbarian conquerors rarely placate their subjects: if they do not accept the national religion, they are hated as heretics or unbelievers; if they employ foreigners to govern the country, they deprive themselves of the skill and experience of native administrators . . . if they maintain peace, the martial virtues of their people will decay and their weapons rust from want of use; if they strive to reign as kings of all races and classes, they risk being repudiated as renegades by their fellow-barbarians, who still enjoy a monopoly of military power and lord it over a nation of slaves.[48]

The Ilkhanate's last Mongol ruler, Ilkhan Abu Said, died in 1335 without an heir.

Native emirs and viziers took control of the Mongol capitals and treasure, while the provinces were seized by pretenders with their private armies. Trade was disrupted and tax collection disintegrated. To avoid the chaos in the Middle East, trading caravans began traveling north of the Caspian Sea, along a new Silk Road that starved the former Mongol territories of revenue. By 1350, the Ilkhanate had passed into history.

While the Yuan dynasty and the Ilkhanate were collapsing, the Chagatai empire of central Asia endured. During this time, another conqueror, modeling himself after Genghis Khan, was born near the city of Samarkand, ruined a century before by Genghis Khan's own armies. Timur the Lame was a Turkish-speaking Mongol who claimed (wrongly) that he was descended from Genghis Khan. Growing wealthy from banditry, he successfully defended his homeland from raids of the Mongols of the eastern steppes.

In the 1390s, Timur raised a huge army and set out from his homeland to conquer the Golden Horde, the Mongol domain ruled by the successors of Batu in Russia and Ukraine. The war destroyed the old Mongol capital on the lower Volga River and eventually allowed the princes of Russia to free themselves of Mongol rule completely. The Mongol dominions of the Golden Horde split into three: the khanates of Kazan, Astrakhan, and the Crimean Peninsula. Russian armies and colonists traveled east across Siberia, southward into the Asian deserts and steppes, and to the borders of Mongolia itself. In 1405, while on an expedition to conquer China, Timur died. The Timurid Empire that he established quickly disintegrated. The Mongol Empire vanished completely.

DRINKING AND THE DECLINE OF THE MONGOL EMPIRE

Overindulgence shortened the life spans of many Mongol rulers who followed Genghis Khan. Ogedei, the son of Genghis Khan, died of heavy drinking in 1241. The next Great Khan, Guyuk, reigned for only two years, from 1246 until 1248. The Ilkhans lived short lives, as did the successors of Kublai Khan in China. Toghan Timur, the longest-lasting of them all, lived to only fifty. According to historian John Masson Smith, in his article "Dietary Decadence and Dynastic Decline in the Mongol Empire," drinking played a key role in the decline of the Mongol Empire:

> Male alcoholism complemented by heavy drinking on the part of Mongol women may have compromised fertility as well as longevity.

A modern-day Mongolian man enjoys a fermented alcoholic beverage.

The corollary of short lifespans was short reigns . . . short reigns, in turn, made for frequent successions, which were often disruptive, since Inner Asian tribal people had no firm rules or principles governing the transmission of chiefly authority . . . the Mongol princes increasingly resorted to force or the threat of force in claiming chieftaincy, and increasingly this armed competition led to military stalemate and political fragmentation. . . . Had the descendants of Chinggis spent less time at the table, they might have lasted longer on the throne, and produced more stable, more capable, and even further-flung government.

Effects of the Mongol Conquest

Although they did not create a lasting empire, Genghis Khan and the Mongols had far-reaching effects on world history. Under Mongol rule, Turkish peoples of central Asia left their homelands and began migrating west, eventually conquering large swaths of the Middle East, Asia Minor, and southeastern Europe and founding the Ottoman Empire. When the crusaders of the Middle East refused to ally themselves with the Mongols against their common Islamic enemies, they assured their own destruction. In 1291, the last crusader fortress, Acre, was captured by the Muslims. The Christian principalities of the Levant vanished, and from this point Islamic states ruled the Middle East.

In China, the Yuan dynasty founded by Kublai Khan united northern and southern China, regions that had long been divided, politically and culturally. Kublai Khan adopted Tibetan Buddhism, converting the Mongols to this faith and making Taoism and Confucianism less important at his court. The administration established by the khan gave China a common system of taxation, land use, and trade, while improving roads, irrigation, and communication. After the Chinese threw off Mongol rule and built the Ming dynasty, China developed into an economic and military superpower in Asia—largely thanks to the efforts of the Yuan emperors to make the country easier to govern.

The Mongol destruction of cities in Persia (modern Iran) and of Baghdad, then the capital of the Islamic world, slowed the many advances in science, mathematics, astronomy, philosophy, and other fields pioneered by Arab and Islamic thinkers.

The religion of Islam went on the defensive; after the demise of Mongol rule, Islamic lands adopted a strict, fundamentalist religion that permitted no dissent and expelled foreign beliefs altogether. In India, the harsh rule of the Mogul kings, descended from Mongol khans but adopting Islam, clashed with the Hinduism that was native to the region. The Moguls were eventually overthrown by Great Britain's colonization of India, but conflict between Muslims and Hindus thrives today throughout the modern, independent nation of India.

In Russia, the two centuries of domination by the Golden Horde left a permanent mark on Russian politics and culture. The princes of Moscow, who threw off the Mongol rulers to become the czars (emperors) of all Russia, adopted from the Mongols an absolutism that allowed Russian czars complete and unquestioned control of the state. Many historians also see Mongol rule echoed in the totalitarianism of the twentieth-century Soviet Union.

In the meantime, the people of Mongolia continued to revere Genghis Khan, whom they consider the founder of their nation. Although Mongolia underwent some industrialization in the twentieth century, many Mongols still live as herders and nomads, belong to close-knit clans, and have little contact with foreign people or culture. The ancient homeland of the Mongol tribe, along the Onon River, became forbidden territory, closed to all outsiders. Writing in 1930, Boris Vladimirtsov described how the banner of Genghis Khan was still revered as the symbol of his authority and spirit: "To this day the Mongols preserve and reverence the White Banner of the *Sulde*, which is the same,

SEARCHING FOR OGEDEI'S PALACES

Ogedei, the son of Genghis Khan, continued the Mongol habit of seasonal migration from his city of Karakorum. In fact, the second Great Khan only lived in Karakorum for a few days every year, in the late spring and early summer. In his essay "Seasonal Migrations of the Mongol Emperors and the Peri-Urban Area of Kharakhorum," Japanese archaeologist Noriyuki Shiraishi traces Ogedei's wanderings during the rest of the year:

> The emperor left Kharakhorum in early spring, travelled north along the Orkhon river, and hunted birds at Doityn Balgas, where he spent the spring. In early summer he went south, going via Kharakhorum, and spent summer in the Khangai Range. Then he moved to the autumn camp and in early winter went south along the Ongi river to spend winter at Shaazan-khot. He probably went hunting in the Gobi area to the south. When spring came he returned north to Kharakhorum.

> Guided by the books of the historians Juvaini and Rashid al-Din, Shiraishi and other archaeologists are currently searching for the remains of these seasonal camps. They face a difficult task. The medieval historians give a variety of names and locations for these places. There are no remains above ground—archaeologists can only trace foundations and, if they are lucky, find and date scattered tiles, pottery fragments, tools, arrowheads, and other small objects. Nevertheless, Shiraishi claims to have found the spring palace in the Arkhangai province of modern Mongolia as well as the winter palace at Shaazan-khot. The summer and fall palaces are still unknown, with their locations only guessed at on Shiraishi's map of Ogedei's restless wanderings.

they believe, that led the armies of Chingis-Khan from victory to victory. They believe that the soul of the great Emperor has itself entered the *sulde* banner, and that he has himself become the guardian-genius of his glorious clan, which to this day governs the Mongols."[49]

A New View of Genghis Khan

The life of Genghis Khan has long fascinated historians, who have found in him two very contradictory aspects: ruthless conqueror and wise, just ruler. For centuries, Genghis Khan and the Mongols were treated as little more than a human plague.

Although their army's power and skill were admired, the Mongols' habit of wholesale massacre made them into the great historical example of unthinking, bloodthirsty barbarians. The fact that the Mongol Empire did not long survive the death of Genghis Khan proved that the Mongol realm was no more than the product of one man's great charisma and ambition.

In the twentieth century, historians generally changed these opinions. In this new view, Genghis Khan was a true revolutionary, who established an important model for the nations and governments that followed his time. His code of law and administration brought a period of stability and peace to much of the world, allowing trade, culture, and communication to flourish along the roads between Europe and Asia. Historian Jack Weatherford advances the idea that the Mongols laid the groundwork for the twenty-first-century world: "In conquering their empire, not only had the Mongols revolutionized warfare, they also created the nucleus of a universal culture . . . it became the foundation for the modern world system with the original Mongol emphases on free commerce, open communication, shared knowledge, secular politics, religious coexistence, international law, and diplomatic immunity."[50] Whether or not the Mongols ushered in modern civilization, the record shows that the realm of Genghis Khan was one of the most innovative in history. The Mongol Empire will likely be a subject of debate and new interpretations for a long time to come.

NOTES

Chapter 1: The Rise of Genghis Khan

1. Quoted in Per Inge Oestman, "Mongol History and Chronology from Ancient Times: The Origin of the Mongols," The Realm of the Mongols. www.coldsiberia.org/webdoc3.htm.
2. Quoted in Paul Ratchnevsky, *Genghis Khan: His Life and Legacy*. Oxford: Blackwell, 1992, p. 7.
3. David Morgan, *The Mongols*. New York: Blackwell, 1986, p. 59.
4. Quoted in Jack Weatherford, *Genghis Khan and the Making of the Modern World*. New York: Crown, 2004, p. 6.
5. Michael Prawdin, *The Mongol Empire: Its Rise and Legacy*. London: Allen and Unwin, 1961, p. 46.
6. Boris Vladimirtsov, *The Life of Chingis Khan*. New York: B. Bloom, 1969, p. 64.
7. Quoted in Ratchnevsky, *Genghis Khan*, p. 187.
8. Quoted in Ratchnevsky, *Genghis Khan*, p. 123.

Chapter 2: An Unstoppable Force: The Mongol Army

9. Richard Hakluyt, *The Principal Navigations, Voyages, Traffiques and Discoveries of the English Nation*. New York:
Dutton, 1927, 1: 91–93, The Medieval Sourcebook. www.fordham.edu/halsall/source/tartars.html.
10. Quoted in Vladimirtsov, *Life of Chingis Khan*, p. 67.
11. Quoted in Vladimirtsov, *Life of Chingis Khan*, p. 68.
12. Timothy May, "Mongol Arms," Explorations in Empire: The Mongols. http://www.accd.edu/sac/history/keller/Mongols/empsub2.html.
13. B.H. Liddell Hart, *Great Captains Unveiled*. Freeport, NY: Books for Libraries, 1967, p. 32.
14. Quoted in John Andrew Boyle, ed., *The Mongol World Empire, 1206–1370*. London: Variorum Reprints, 1977, p. 5.
15. Morgan, *Mongols*, p. 35.

Chapter 3: The Code of the Mongols

16. Ratchnevsky, *Genghis Khan*, p. 167.
17. J.J. Saunders, *The History of the Mongol Conquests*. London: Routledge and K. Paul, 1971, p. 66.
18. Michael Hoang, *Genghis Khan*. New York: New Amsterdam, 1991, p. 154.
19. Vladimirtsov, *Life of Chingis Khan*, p. 66.
20. Saunders, *History of the Mongol Conquests*, p. 65.

21. Weatherford, *Genghis Khan and the Making of the Modern World*, p. 101.

Chapter 4: The Life of the Mongols

22. Quoted in Ratchnevsky, *Genghis Khan*, p. 21.
23. Quoted in Oestman, "Mongol History and Chronology from Ancient Times."
24. Rashid al-Din, *Collection of Histories*. New York: Columbia University Press, 1971, p. 65.
25. Weatherford, *Genghis Khan and the Making of the Modern World*, p. 125.
26. Milton Rugoff, *Marco Polo's Adventures in China*. New York: Harper & Row, 1964, pp. 99–100.
27. Quoted in Prawdin, *Mongol Empire*, p. 95.
28. E.D. Phillips, *The Mongols*. New York: Praeger, 1969, p. 27.
29. Quoted in John Masson Smith, "Dietary Decadence and Dynastic Decline in the Mongol Empire." http://afe. easia.columbia.edu/mongols/pastoral/ masson_smith.pdf.
30. William of Rubruck, *William of Rubruck's Account of the Mongols*. http://depts.washington.edu/uwch/sil kroad/texts/rubruck.html
31. Rashid al-Din, *Successors of Genghis Khan*, p. 65.

Chapter 5: Shamanism and the Eternal Sky

32. Saunders, *History of the Mongol Conquests*, p. 68.
33. Hoang, *Genghis Khan*, p. 157.

34. Peter Brent, *Genghis Khan: The Rise, Authority and Decline of Mongol Power*. New York: McGraw-Hill, 1976, p. 30.
35. Stanley Stewart, *In the Empire of Genghis Khan: A Journey Among Nomads*. Guilford, CT: Lyons Press, 2002, p. 125.
36. William of Rubruck, *William of Rubruck's Account of the Mongols*.
37. Quoted in Boyle, *Mongol World Empire*, p. 145.
38. Robert Guisepi, The Mongols, http://history_world.org/mongol_ empire.html.

Chapter 6: The Decline of the Mongol Empire

39. Brent, *Genghis Khan*, p. 110.
40. Phillips, *Mongols*, p. 69.
41. William of Rubruck, *William of Rubruck's Account of the Mongols*.
42. al-Din, *Collection of Histories*, p. 64
43. Morgan, *Mongols*, p. 199.
44. C.P. Fitzgerald, *The Horizon History of China*. New York: American Heritage, 1969, p. 247.
45. Brent, *Genghis Khan*, p. 159.
46. Brent, *Genghis Khan*, p. 163.
47. Phillips, *Mongols*, pp. 139–140.
48. Saunders, *History of the Mongol Conquests*, p. 140.
49. Vladimirtsov, *Life of Chingis Khan*, p. 65.
50. Weatherford, *Genghis Khan and the Making of the Modern World*, p. 233.

FOR FURTHER READING

James Chambers, *The Devil's Horsemen: The Mongol Invasion of Europe*. New York: Atheneum, 1979. Writing from the Mongol perspective, the author provides a colorful description of the Mongol encounter with the West, when the army of the steppes encountered medieval European arms and tactics and invaded Poland and Hungary.

Richard A. Gabriel, *Subotai the Valiant: Genghis Khan's Greatest General*. Westport, CT: Praeger, 2004. The first English biography of Genghis Khan's leading general reveals how the Mongols used speed, maneuver, and surprise in their successful battle tactics and how many of Subedei's own doctrines of battle have been taken up in modern warfare.

Miriam Greenblatt, *Genghis Khan and the Mongol Empire*. New York: Benchmark, 2002. The biography of Genghis Khan as a background to a more general discussion of Mongol social conditions, culture, and religion.

René Grousset, *Conqueror of the World*. New York: Orion, 1966. A prominent art historian explores the conquests of Genghis Khan and the Mongol influence on Chinese culture and society.

Paul Kahn and Francis Woodman Cleaves, *Secret History of the Mongols: The Origin of Chingis Khan*. Boston: Cheng & Tsui, 1998. A rendering of the Mongols' thirteenth-century chronicle *The Secret History* into a narrative poem in modern English. The book provides maps, lineage charts, and a useful glossary.

Luc Kwanten, *Imperial Nomads: A History of Central Asia, 500–1500*. Philadelphia: University of Pennsylvania Press, 1979. A history of the migrations of the steppe nomads, useful for background information on the Mongols and the effect of Genghis Khan's conquest on central Asia.

Owen Lattimore and Eleanor Lattimore, eds., *Silks, Spices and Empire: Asia Seen Through the Eyes of Its Discoverers*. New York: Delacorte, 1968. An interesting collection of travel writings from many different periods, in which first-person narratives describe the fascinating mysteries of Asia.

John Man, *Genghis Khan: Life, Death, and Resurrection*. New York: Thomas Dunne, 2005. The author relates the story of Genghis Khan's rise and conquest of an empire and describes his own journeys to Mongolia's "sacred mountain" of Burkhun Khaldun, the possible burial site of the Universal Ruler.

David R. Ringrose, *Expansion and Global Interaction: 1200–1700*. New York: Longman, 2001. A historian of Spain, Ringrose explores the increasingly interdependent world that was largely brought into existence by the Mongol conquests of the early thirteenth century.

Morris Rossabi, *Kublai Khan: His Life and Times*. Berkeley: University of California Press, 1988. A well-written, useful biography of Kublai Khan, one of the very few complete treatments of this important leader written in English. The early chapters deal with the rise of the Mongol Empire.

Milton Rugoff, *Marco Polo's Adventures in China*. New York: Harper & Row, 1964. A book for young readers on the travels of a thirteenth-century Italian merchant through the domains of Kublai Khan.

Tim Severin, *In Search of Genghis Khan: An Exhilarating Journey on Horseback Across the Steppes of Mongolia*. Lanham, MD: Cooper Square, 2003. An often-reprinted documentary of the author's journey on horseback through modern Mongolia, in which he finds traces of the ancient Mongol lifestyle in his encounters with contemporary Mongol herders, guides, and traveling companions.

Bertold Spuler, *History of the Mongols*. Berkeley: University of California Press, 1972. A German scholar's account of the Mongol Empire.

Robert Taylor, *Life in Genghis Khan's Mongolia*. San Diego: Lucent Books, 2001. A useful, interesting description of the physical and social environment of Mongolia during Genghis Khan's time.

WORKS CONSULTED

Books

Rashid al-Din, *Collection of Histories*. New York: Columbia University Press, 1971. In the late thirteenth century, the Persian historian who served as a minister in the Ilkhanate was commissioned to write this chronicle of the Mongol Empire under the descendants of Genghis Khan.

Christopher Atwood, *Encyclopedia of Mongolia and the Mongol Empire*. New York: Facts On File, 2004. A useful and comprehensive reference source on Mongol history, religion, culture, art, and politics.

John Andrew Boyle, ed., *The Mongol World Empire, 1206–1370*. London: Variorum Reprints, 1977. A collection of reprinted journal articles by various authors on scholarly questions and debates.

Peter Brent, *Genghis Khan: The Rise, Authority and Decline of Mongol Power*. New York: McGraw-Hill, 1976. A complete, vividly written account of the Mongol Empire, from origins to collapse, in which the author speculates on the motivations, events, conversations, and personalities of the leading figures of the period.

C.P. Fitzgerald. *The Horizon History of China*. New York: American Heritage, 1969. A comprehensive overview of Chinese political and artistic history, well illustrated and suitable for readers exploring the field for the first time.

Michael Hoang, *Genghis Khan*. New York: New Amsterdam, 1991. A French journalist explores the life and campaigns of Genghis Khan, giving good insight into military strategy and tactics of the Mongol army.

Richard Hakluyt, *The Principal Navigations, Voyages, Traffiques and Discoveries of the English Nation*. New York: Dutton, 1927, 1:91–93, The Medieval Sourcebook. www.fordham.edu/halsall/source/tartars.html. This online page offers a brief quotation from a sixteenth-century English historian's account of the medieval "Tartars." The Internet Medieval Sourcebook is an encyclopedic collection of primary source documents dealing with medieval Europe.

B.H. Liddell Hart, *Great Captains Unveiled*. Freeport, NY: Books for Libraries, 1967. The British military historian analyzes the careers of six military commanders, beginning with Genghis Khan and Subedei, the general who led the Mongol reconnaissance into the Caucasus Mountains and Russia.

David Morgan, *The Mongols*. New York: Blackwell, 1986. An excellent introduction to the study of Mongol history, in which the author describes the limited sources of information available and the many debates and controversies that still surround Genghis Khan and the empire he built.

E.D. Phillips, *The Mongols*. New York: Praeger, 1969. A detailed, scholarly description of Mongol history, culture, and society that is fairly accessible for readers coming to the subject for the first time.

Marco Polo, *The Travels*. New York: Penguin, 1958. The Italian merchant describes his journey across Asia, including his experiences in Kublai Khan's China. Although this book is the most famous travel book in history, the author displays a vivid imagination and historians are doubtful about many of the places, events, and people he describes.

Michael Prawdin, *The Mongol Empire: Its Rise and Legacy*. London: Allen and Unwin, 1961. A detailed history of the Mongol Empire, relying on contemporary accounts and *The Secret History* to render a speculative eyewitness account.

Paul Ratchnevsky, *Genghis Khan: His Life and Legacy*. Oxford: Blackwell, 1992. One of the most authoritative biographies of Genghis Khan, drawing on all literary and historical sources.

J.J. Saunders, *The History of the Mongol Conquests*. London: Routledge and K. Paul, 1971. A straightforward, detailed history of the Mongol Empire, dealing thoroughly with Genghis Khan's successors in the Middle East, Russia, and central Asia.

Stanley Stewart, *In the Empire of Genghis Khan: A Journey Among Nomads*. Guilford, CT: Lyons Press, 2002. The author journeys through modern Mongolia in search of cultural and religious traces of the medieval Mongol Empire.

Boris Vladimirtsov, *The Life of Chingis Khan*. New York: B. Bloom, 1969. A Russian historian's biography of Genghis Khan and a detailed analysis of the Mongol conquest of the steppes of what is now southern Russia and Ukraine.

Jack Weatherford, *Genghis Khan and the Making of the Modern World*. New York: Crown, 2004. A readable, strongly opinionated account of Mongol history, advancing the view of the Mongols as tolerant and progressive rulers and their empire as a foundation of the modern world as we know it.

Periodicals

Noriyuki Shiraishi, "Seasonal Migrations of the Mongol Emperors and the Peri-Urban Area of Kharakhorum," *The International Journal of Asian Studies*, January 2004.

Internet Sources

Robert Guisepi, "The Mongol Empire," The Mongols, http://history-world.org/mongol_empire.htm.

Timothy May, "Mongol Arms," Explorations in Empire: The Mongols. www.accd.edu/sac/history/keller/Mongols/empsub2.html.

Per Inge Oestman, "Mongol History and Chronology from Ancient Times: The Origin of the Mongols," from The Realm of the Mongols, www.coldsiberia.org/webdoc3.htm.

John Masson Smith, "Dietary Decadence and Dynastic Decline in the Mongol Empire." http://afe.easia.columbia.edu/mongols/pastoral/masson_smith.pdf.

William of Rubruck, *William of Rubruck's Account of the Mongols*. http://depts.washington.edu/uwch/silkroad/texts/rubruck.html.

INDEX

polygamy, 55–56

ponies, 60

Prawdin, Michael, 18

quriltais (assemblies), 19, 43, 49, 79–81

raiding, 12, 15, 53, 55

Ratchnevsky, Paul, 14, 39

religion(s)

    debate about virtues of different, 24, 69

    in Ilkhanate, 86, 90

    of Mongols, 71–72, 74–76, 80–81

    position of khan and, 19, 20

    tolerance of all, 46, 65, 76–77

Rockhill, W.W., 42

Rugoff, Milton, 55, 56

Russia, 90, 92

Said, Ilkhan Abu, 90

Samarkand (Khwarezm), 23, 25

Saunders, J.J., 39, 44, 65, 90

scapulimacy, 69, 71

scimitars, 26

"Seasonal Migrations of the Mongol Emperors and the Peri-Urban Area of Kharakhorum" (Shiraishi), 93

Secret History of the Mongols, The (book), 11, 13

shamans, 66, 68–69, 71, 72, 90

Shankh Monastery (Mongolia), 34

Shiraishi, Noriyuki, 93

Siberia, 15

siege engines, 27–28

Silk Road, 23, 90

slavery, 16, 41, 42, 57

Smith, John Mason, 91

society

    leadership in, 15, 16

    marriage and position in, 55

    obedience in, 43

    structure of, 12–13, 50

Soviet Union, 11, 34, 92
    see also Russia

steppe tribes, 12, 15

Stewart, Stanley, 68

Subedei, 34

sulde (banner), 34, 92–93

PICTURE CREDITS

ABOUT THE AUTHOR

Tom Streissguth was born in Washington, D.C., and grew up in Minneapolis. He attended Yale University, where he majored in music and also studied history, languages, and English language and literature. He has worked as an editor, teacher, and journalist and has traveled in Europe, the Middle East, Latin America, and Asia. Tom has written more than sixty books of nonfiction for young readers for Lerner, Oliver, Facts On File, Enslow, Lucent/Greenhaven, Millbrook, and Marshall Cavendish. These include biographies, history books, geography books, and several titles on current political affairs and social issues. He has two daughters, Louison and Adele, who are attending school in Sarasota, Florida.